Praise for
World Wide Search

"Cheryl Green gives some hard facts on Internet dating, a phenomenon that's clearly on the rise. In *World Wide Search,* she shows Christians how they can best navigate and make good use of its possibilities."
—TOMMY NELSON, author of *The Book of Romance*

"This book is a necessity for anyone who chooses to socialize in cyber-space. Biblical standards for relationships and great advice on how to master the intricacies of connecting online are just a few of the benefits of reading *World Wide Search.* There is also plenty of just plain good advice for proceeding toward a healthy, committed relationship."
—MICHELLE MCKINNEY HAMMOND, author of *Sassy, Single, and Satisfied* and *In Search of the Proverbs 31 Man*

"Cheryl Green challenges readers to examine their own make-up and motivation in pursuit of relationships, and she provides guidelines and guardrails for those who choose to use electronic communication in the process. *World Wide Search* provides positive, protective, and practical steps for seeking God's guidance in finding the love of your life."
—DR. JACK GRAHAM, pastor of Prestonwood Baptist Church in Dallas and president of the Southern Baptist Convention

"I constantly counsel singles in their search for love, and this book is required reading! Finding love in the 21st century requires both the Bible and the Internet, and Cheryl Green has provided the guide that every single should follow. The success stories of believers who have found love online dismiss the notion that the Internet is not for Christians."
—DR. SHERON C. PATTERSON, author of *The Love Clinic*

"*World Wide Search* provides a compass for those thinking about navigating a relationship on the Internet. Cheryl Green's advice is beware, be educated, and be prepared. You may be just one click away from a match made in heaven."

—CHUCK BORSELLINO, PHD, PSYD; cohost of *At Home—Live!*

World
Wide
Se@rch

World Wide Se@rch

The Savvy Christian's Guide to Online Dating

cheryl green

WATERBROOK
PRESS

WORLD WIDE SEARCH
PUBLISHED BY WATERBROOK PRESS
2375 Telstar Drive, Suite 160
Colorado Springs, Colorado 80920
A division of Random House, Inc.

ISBN 1-57856-883-8

Library of Congress Cataloging-in-Publication Data

Green, Chery, 1970–
World wide search : the savvy Christian's guide to online dating / Cheryl Green.—1st ed.
    p. cm.
  Includes bibliographical references.
  ISBN 1-57856-883-8
  1. Online dating. 2. Courtship. 3. Christian life. I. Title.
HQ801.82.G74 2005
646.7'7'02854678—dc22   2004004269

Printed in the United States of America
2004—First Edition

10 9 8 7 6 5 4 3 2 1

For those who have given up—
With God, there is always hope.

Contents

Part 1: Before You Create a Screen Name

Part 2: Online Dating Secrets Revealed

Part 3: You Met Someone Special—Now What?

Acknowledgments

To my WaterBrook family—thank you for believing in this project and being such a professional and godly group of people. Ron, God blessed me with an encouraging and affirming editor who made the entire process a growth experience.

To my family—thank you for putting up with my absence while I completed yet another labor of love.

To Robin, Jim, Joe, and Shannon—once again, thank you for being the wise counselors you have always been in my life.

To Lisa, Lisa, and Debbie—thanks for putting up with my bouncing ideas off you and for giving me your honest advice.

To Valerie—thank you for recognizing the timing for this project and helping find a good home for this book at WaterBrook.

To all the people who have shared their stories and insights—thank you for being so transparent and willing to help others. I pray that God will bless each of you in your relationships.

Thank you, heavenly Father, for the blessings and hope in all things found in your Son, Jesus Christ.

Online Dating in the Real World

This Isn't Your Parents' Version of a Blind Date

Angela, a thirty-one-year-old art director living in California, checked out an online dating site after a painful breakup. Three of her girl-friends had found their spouses online, and they urged her to give it a try.

Even with their encouragement, however, Angela was reluctant. She was still hurting from her breakup, and she doubted that she was a good candidate for finding a match online. In fact, as a breast-cancer survivor who'd had a double mastectomy, Angela was losing hope that she'd ever find a man who would want to marry her.

No one who met her would ever guess that Angela harbored such doubts. She was a lively, attractive professional who was active in her church. But inside, she felt like damaged goods. One night, while surfing the Internet, she took a chance and joined an online Christian singles community. After reading several posts on the message board, Angela realized that other singles facing bigger challenges than hers had found "the one" through online dating. So Angela decided to post her profile.

Five hundred miles away, Jerry was checking out available singles on the Internet. A forty-three-year-old divorced high-school coach and single parent of two small children, he had been online for more than a year without much success. He lived in a small town with few singles in his age

group, and he didn't have much money to support a long-distance relationship. "I thought I would find matches much quicker than I did," he
says. "It was like I was wasting my time and money because it was taking
too long."

The day Angela uploaded her profile was the same day Jerry planned
to take his down. But he decided to do one last search of new profiles, and
Angela's was the last one out of twenty. He liked what he saw, and just an
hour after Angela posted her profile, Jerry's e-mail arrived. "He wrote so
well, and he complimented me on my profile," Angela recalls. "In two
days I felt like we had been friends forever."

Angela and Jerry spent hours chatting online, and within a few weeks
they had moved to talking on the telephone. It wasn't long after they had
exchanged photos that Jerry was ready to spend his savings to visit Angela
in California.

"I was scared she might not feel the same way, so I held off asking if
she was okay with a face-to-face meeting," he says. "One day, though, I
couldn't take it anymore and told her how strongly I felt for her. I said that
I needed to visit her and move the relationship to another level."

Upon receiving this news, Angela froze with fear. Was she setting herself up for more rejection? She stopped responding to Jerry's e-mails,
instant messages, and phone calls. He knew he had pushed too soon for
an in-person meeting, so he apologized through e-mails and telephone
messages. Angela sought advice from a friend who scolded her for not
answering Jerry's messages. The friend encouraged her to trust God
enough to make herself vulnerable.

Angela called Jerry and apologized for her behavior. She also told him
about her breast cancer and was surprised by his understanding and
acceptance. They arranged to meet in person, and a few weeks after their
first meeting, Angela met Jerry's children as well. To say they had good

chemistry is an understatement. A year after meeting each other online, Angela and Jerry were married.

"I still laugh at how my impatience nearly kept me from meeting Angie," recalls Jerry. "And then my pushing for a meeting too soon nearly pushed her away. Then she got scared because she thought I wouldn't love her after finding out about her breast cancer. But God orchestrated this thing.... He brought us together against all the odds."

God used the Internet and two honest and open Christians to write a great ending to this love story—cyberspace style.

PRACTICE THE RIGHT SKILLS

You may have heard of success stories similar to Angela and Jerry's, and you may be either dating online or thinking about giving it a try. What I didn't tell you is that both Angela and Jerry went online with the right skills and the necessary offline support. Jerry had been dating online for a year or more, but because of limited finances and his young children, he only pursued matches who lived nearby. Angela was new to Internet dating, but she listened to the advice of girlfriends who were online-dating veterans. Both Angela and Jerry practiced skills that helped them every step of the way.

People who date aren't all looking for the same thing. Some singles just want something to do on Friday nights, while others are serious about a lifelong commitment. But for the purposes of this book, we'll define *dating* as the process of seeking someone to marry. Christian singles tend to share a strong desire for a lifelong bond. If you want a casual relationship, go to the secular dating sites.

So, with the stated goal of seeking a marriage partner, let's consider the online skills you need to develop. Many Christians begin dating online after doing nothing more than hoping and praying for success.

So it's understandable that they often feel overwhelmed or confused about the process. Some succeed in spite of their mistakes, but others become discouraged—or, worse, they are snared by the temptations that proliferate online.

Avoid the traps and unnecessary discouragement by developing the right skills from the start. As you practice the skills discussed in this book, pray constantly, align your efforts with God's will, and relate to others according to His standards. Moving forward in this way will maximize your chances for success in finding your best match.

The Next Step

In the chapters that follow, you'll find advice and valuable insights from savvy veterans of online dating that will provide you with the knowledge and support you need. I am a Christian single on the same journey you are making. Although I am not married yet, I have dated several Christian men I met online. I have also made scores of friends from all over the world.

We all share a common bond—and a common challenge. Dating is more complicated for us than it was for previous generations. Fewer of us are marrying right out of high school or college, many of us have demanding careers or other life circumstances that make it hard to meet like-minded singles, and more of us are becoming single again through divorce. Plus, with the increase in average life expectancy, many of us are becoming single late in life after the death of a spouse. We also live in a much more mobile society in which we have weaker social bonds and less of a sense of community.

The Internet is especially useful if your circumstances limit your social networks. Singles in demanding professions or who work nontraditional hours, those who live in rural areas or small towns, as well as those who attend churches with small numbers of singles find online dating to be a welcome resource. Once a person is in the work world, he or she may be surrounded by married colleagues or by singles who are much older or much younger, don't share the same faith or values, or are available but aren't seeking a committed relationship. For many of us, the traditional social networks of friends, family, and familiar church settings have lost their effectiveness in connecting us with other singles.

I have encountered these challenges, and after years of moderating a large online Christian singles community on *yahoo.com*, I know I'm not alone. Thousands of singles interact online by posting messages and using chat rooms. There they share their personal stories, including their joyful accounts of dating successes and sometimes their painful tales of disappointment and heartbreak. I wrote this book because I want you to enjoy the former and avoid the latter.

Proverbs 17:24 states, "A discerning man keeps wisdom in view, but a fool's eyes wander to the ends of the earth." I created this guidebook to help you at each stage of your online journey so you can avoid wandering all over cyberspace. The skills, interactive devices, advice, and support you'll find in this book will help you from the time you post your profile, to your first introduction to a potential match, to your first in-person date, to the point of deciding whether to make the relationship exclusive.

Online dating expands our social network in ways that transcend time constraints, location, and other limitations of everyday life. It's not a cure-all, but if you develop the right skills, it can be a welcome and effective tool.

EVERYTHING CHANGES—AND NOTHING CHANGES

In many ways, a lot has changed in how people seek out their mates. But in other ways, it's exactly the same. Thousands of years ago, Abraham's chief servant traveled by camel from Canaan to his master's homeland to find a wife for Abraham's son Isaac. The servant approached his task prayerfully: "O LORD…if you will, please grant success to the journey on which I have come" (Genesis 24:42). God did grant him success by revealing that Rebekah was His choice for Isaac.

Today the servant would ditch the smelly camel and the hot, dusty travel. Instead, he might boot up his computer and search profiles to find the best match for Isaac. Actually, Isaac could easily launch the search on his own. While the tools have changed dramatically, one factor remains the same: God never changes. We begin the process in prayer, and we remain in prayer throughout as we seek God's direction.

If you are dating online or considering an Internet search for your best match, you're part of a growing multitude. More than 45 million people[1] have visited as many as 2,500 matchmaking sites on the Internet.[2] Nearly 6 million Americans have used the Internet to find a mate,[3] and a growing number of these are Christians.

But there is no consensus within the Christian community on using the Internet as a matchmaking tool. Some Christians put the Internet on par with past generations meeting like-minded singles at a church picnic or potluck dinner or a dance or community social. Others feel the Internet is in a different league altogether. Critics argue that there are too many opportunities for deception when people meet online. Supporters counter with the argument that deception began long before there was a World Wide Web. In fact, it began long before Abraham's servant set out to find a bride for Isaac. People can be just as dishonest when talking to you in person as they can be from a computer keyboard. Some people may have dishonorable motives, but there are plenty of good and honest people in cyberspace. Furthermore, God still guides us and answers our prayers. He gives wisdom to those who ask for it (see James 1:5).

We desperately need God's wisdom. Regardless of the many advantages of online dating, we've all heard the horror stories—the accounts of lying, scams, pornography, and a host of other traps. Perhaps you remember news reports of the military officer who proposed marriage to fifty different women after wooing them online.[4] His scam came to light early enough for the women to get out with nothing worse than bruised dignity. These women got caught up in the romance and were lulled into thinking they'd found their soul mate. So slap yourself out of Disneyland if you feel like planning a wedding after a few e-mails or chats with someone you haven't met in person. You'll thank me later.

We're naive if we overlook the significant challenges and a few real dangers associated with dating online. When you're online you can never be fully certain who the other person *really* is. But even if you meet someone in a reading group, at the health club, or at a church singles event, you don't know who the person really is. Many of the risks are the same whether you meet in person or online. However, savvy online daters stress that those who understand the rules and practice the right skills will significantly reduce the risks of being conned. (For an in-depth discussion of Internet safety, see chapter 9.)

When appropriate safeguards are in place and you are seeking God's direction, the Internet is a viable dating option. Rather than limiting a search to one church, or even one city, a single today can search worldwide for God's blessing of a mate. If you have limited time to pursue social contacts, you might find the Internet to be just the tool you need. Likewise, if you broke up with a dating partner and don't know how to get back into the dating scene, this could be a useful approach. Even if you are merely curious about online dating or are definitely interested but unsure how to begin, the advice in this book will give you a great start.

SET REALISTIC GOALS

The Christians you will meet in this book share the secrets to their successes in online dating. And not all of them define *success* solely in terms of marriage. Success may include befriending other Christian singles to enlarge your social network and support base or getting to know other singles in a way that helps you clarify the attributes in a spouse that are most important to you.

Some research suggests that solid online relationships that make it to marriage fare better than those developed from chance meetings offline.[5] People share four times more personal information in online conversations than in person, and as a result of this openness online, relationships have the potential to provide those who make it to the altar with a solid foundation for effective communication in marriage.[6] However, research also reveals that 75 percent of online relationships never reach the point of an in-person date.[7] One of several reasons for this is that many people go online without first developing the appropriate skills, goals, or patience to conduct effective searches.

Still, more and more Christian singles are logging on each day. You just have to know where they are, how to meet them, and how to maximize the benefits and minimize the risks of using the Internet in your quest. Since Christians remain divided over the appropriateness of online dating, you need to examine your own convictions before logging on. Step back from the computer, ask God for insight and clarity, and then ask yourself what you really believe about dating online.

If you have doubts about whether you are doing the right thing, please don't pursue online dating. The apostle Paul addressed the Roman Christians who were passing judgment on each other over whether it was a sin to eat food considered unclean by Jewish standards. He concluded that Christians should act on what they believed brought glory to God, even if they differed on the question of eating meat that had been sacrificed to idols (see Romans 14:1-23; 1 Corinthians 8:1-13). If someone held his or her beliefs for the glory of God, Paul did not condemn that person. However, each person was warned to be "fully convinced in his own mind," since "blessed is the man who does not condemn himself by what he approves" (Romans 14:5,22). So don't enter cyberspace filled with doubt, shame, or fear.

But if you are ready to begin your online journey, then set out with a prayer. Use the following prayer as a guide or pour out your heart to God in your own words so that you can begin this journey with confidence.

Heavenly Father, You know the desires of my heart. Please bless my efforts as I go online. Help me to never get out of step with You. Help me to let go and allow You to remain in control of my life. Father, please let Your hand be with me and keep me from harm. At the same time, Father, please help me not to be the cause of pain or harm to others. In everything I do, I pray that it will always be to your glory. In Jesus's name I pray these things. Amen.

PART 1

Before You Create
a Screen Name

"For I know the plans I have for you,"
declares the LORD, "plans to prosper you
and not to harm you, plans to give you
hope and a future. Then you will call upon
me and come and pray to me, and I will
listen to you. You will seek me and find
me when you seek me with all your heart."

—JEREMIAH 29:11-13

One

What You Need Going In

Give Yourself the Best Chance for Success

Let's get real about online dating right from the start. It won't solve all of your dating problems, and it sure isn't the easy way to find a date.

In the interest of full disclosure, I feel compelled to bring up two basic caveats. First, online dating has nothing in common with Hollywood movies or effortless Disneyland romance. Listen, I love the movie *You've Got Mail.* Who doesn't? But face it, Meg and Tom were parroting lines from a script. In real life a really cute Meg Ryan clone doesn't just stumble into an engaging e-mail relationship with a clever, charming Tom Hanks look-alike. It doesn't happen because we don't have a copy of the screenplay, and relationships like that just don't magically happen. But Tom and Meg sure make a cute fantasy couple.

The second reality is that online dating takes place in the real world with all of the real-world challenges and limitations. Online dating takes a lot of work and hours of effort. And not everyone will walk away with a wedding ring. If you have been hurt or disappointed in traditional dating, don't expect the Internet to transform your social life. It won't. In fact, cyberspace will actually add a few new wrinkles to the process.

Many disillusioned people thought online dating was a guarantee of success. They assumed that all they needed was access to millions of available singles and they would soon find "the one." If that's you, stop and take a deep breath.

Online dating appeals to many because it's convenient—you can date from home and on your own schedule. The process is also attractive to many because it allows people to connect with an astounding number of singles.

But it's *not easy*. Online dating is incredibly time consuming. Just getting everything set up, creating your profile, and finding the best online singles communities and matchmaking sites takes preparation, effort, and time. The skills you will learn in this book will put you ahead of the game and will help you avoid confusion, disappointment, and hurt. But since online dating is still evolving, there are no hard and fast rules for success. Much of what you learn about the process you will learn as you go. Just make sure you don't have to learn things the hard way.

The Advantages of Dating Online

Online communication has several clear advantages. First, people who date online are forced to talk about matters of substance earlier in the relationship. You spend less time in small talk and instead get to know the other person's values, beliefs, and attitudes early in the relationship. So, in most cases, you won't spend months developing a relationship only to discover later that the two of you are incompatible.

A second big advantage is captured in the slogan "falling in love from the inside out," used by many online dating sites. When dating online, people get to know each other's hearts without the distraction of outward appearances. Singles who don't match the culture's definition of *beautiful people* due to body type, age, disability, or income level can meet people who get to know who they *really* are without being biased by cultural standards. The Internet gives everyone a fair shot at being known for who they are inside.

Several other benefits serve as big selling points for online dating:

- *You don't have to rush.* As you meet people online, you can keep things low-key as you get to know several people by e-mail. There is no obligation to quickly narrow the field to just one person. You can also control the pace of conversations, and you can choose when you'll respond, particularly when corresponding by e-mail. You can take your time and answer questions thoughtfully, communicating at your own pace.

- *You don't feel as pressured.* At the start of an online friendship, you can concentrate on communication without the distractions of what you'll wear, where you should meet, and what you should do together on a date. Instead, you start at the best place for developing any relationship: emphasizing open, honest communication. Plus, because you're writing . er than speaking, you can be more detailed and precise in online conversations.

- *There is time to reflect and gain perspective.* You can save your e-mail conversations and reread them later. This is helpful when you sense good chemistry and you need to slow down and make sure you're not reading too much into the other person's messages. Also, you can use previous e-mails to ensure the person is telling you the truth. Is he or she consistent over time in descriptions, stories, viewpoints, and personal details?

- *You have access to an incredible number of singles.* No longer are you limited to meeting others only in your own city or region. The Internet expands your social network to include the entire world. That may appeal to some people and horrify others. Remember, you're still in control of how much you enlarge your

territory. If you want to limit your search to people in your own
ZIP code, you can.

- *You are free to be yourself.* If you typically grow quiet when you're
  in a group or an unfamiliar social setting, online dating frees
  you to really express yourself. By communicating in writing, you
  can allow your true self to emerge. Some may argue that people
  who communicate by e-mail aren't really being their true selves,
  but are instead presenting an idealized version of themselves.
  Some of that may be true, but it's in your best interest to present
  the real you online. If you meet a match offline and stray too
  far from the persona you presented online, you can kiss that
  relationship good-bye. So don't pretend to be someone else; be
  yourself.

THE LIMITATIONS OF ONLINE DATING

Although there are clear advantages to meeting people over the Internet,
it's important to keep in mind the limitations. You're meeting strangers by
e-mail or in a chat room, and you don't have the visual clues that come
naturally with in-person conversation. Here are a few of the limitations to
be aware of.

- *You can't see the other person.* I know, this one's obvious. But think
  about the implications. Not being able to see and hear each other
  when you converse can leave you vulnerable to the other person's
  lying about who he or she is. The e-mail says he's twenty-eight
  and athletic when he's actually fifty-eight and obese. But that's
  not all. E-mail is silent, just like letters. You miss out on nuances,
  since written words leave out much of the information that is
  communicated in spoken words. The human voice communicates
  meaning through pitch, volume, tone, inflection, and the pace of

speaking. Even if you do voice-chat online, other nonverbal cues are absent that would normally supply information about a person's emotions and intent. That is, unless you're using Web cams or even video phones for a chat.

- *You might be tempted to read into a message.* When you rely on text-only communication, it's easy to hear what you want to hear. You can assume meaning that's not really there and hinder the relationship by falling into miscommunication and misunderstanding. "I was happy to receive your recent e-mail" could mean that the person was dying to hear from you, or simply that he or she is politely acknowledging receipt of your last message. It could even mean that the person sent you a form letter. So take e-mail messages at face value.

- *You may fall victim to romantic fantasies.* Online communication tends to encourage a fantasy element in relationships. The person receiving a message may reshape the image of the sender to fit an imagined ideal. Likewise, the person sending a message may present an idealized persona rather than a realistic picture of who he or she really is. Online communication often frees people to present themselves as wittier, more outgoing, or more creative than they really are in person. But if these qualities don't come through when you meet a match in real life, you may be disappointed. Sure, there is little you can do if the other person goes all Disney on you, but don't fuel the madness by getting swept away with the rush of romance.

- *You'll encounter widely contrasting backgrounds and experiences.* Since the Internet expands the universe of available singles, it's likely that you and your match will share very little common history. When our parents and grandparents were dating, they often had much in common already when they began a relationship.

They may have grown up in the same city, attended the same
school or college, and even known some of the same people.
That's the strength of meeting people through mutual acquaintances, family, church, or work. With online dating, however, you
will share far fewer of these natural links.

- *You don't have the benefit of doing things together.* With an in-person
relationship, couples spend a lot of time talking, of course. But
they also do a lot of talking while they're *doing* something
together—playing tennis or participating in a ministry project
or simply going for a walk or a drive. By engaging in these kinds
of activities, they also enjoy shared experiences that help build a
relationship. Shared activity online is limited to Internet games,
such as chess or dominoes, or building a joint Web site. As great as
these moments can be and as much as you may feel intense chemistry online, they need to be verified through in-person activities.
You get to know a person on a deeper level when you do things
together in various settings, circumstances, and emotional states.
That's when you can observe who the other person *really* is.

A HIGH-TECH BLIND DATE

Before getting into the practical skills that will increase your chances for
success, I would like you to consider one last issue: the reactions of those
around you. Many in your family or church or circle of acquaintances
may have doubts about the propriety of dating on the Internet. Some
people might try to convince you that what you're doing is not condoned
by the Bible. This attitude comes partly from a lack of familiarity with the
technology, but there is also a certain bias against online dating—as if it's
less legitimate than meeting others in person.

Don't even try to change other people's minds. They'll believe what they want to believe, and you'll just get hurt and angry trying to change their minds. It's more beneficial to spend your time dealing with your own feelings about online dating. If you feel ashamed about meeting people online, then you may be driven to go online secretly. This will prevent you from gaining needed outside perspective and support from fair-minded friends and mentors. (Remember, we've already shut our ears to the busybodies and the critics.) You need objective, trustworthy offline support from start to finish. If you find an online relationship that starts to become more serious, you'll need a sounding board who isn't biased or emotionally invested. If you fail to rely on offline support, you'll put yourself at risk for disappointment, hurt, and even potential danger.

The following quiz will show how comfortable you are with online dating. Circle the response that most closely describes your feelings. To get a feel for where you stand, score 2 points for every True response, 1 point for every Sort of True response, and 0 points for every False response. At the end, add up the points for your final score.

1. Online dating is worse than being set up on a blind date.

   True   Sort of True   False

2. Online dating is for those who are socially inept and/or uncomfortable with "real" relationships.

   True   Sort of True   False

3. You can't create real relationships online. Online dating feeds only fantasy relationships.

   True   Sort of True   False

4. People who use the Internet to meet other singles are desperate for a date.

   True   Sort of True   False

5. The Internet is not a proper way for Christians to meet others when looking for a spouse.

   True   Sort of True   False

6. Christians should limit their search for a spouse to church singles' groups and meeting others through friends and family members.

   True   Sort of True   False

7. If you get involved in online dating, you are inviting trouble from predators, perverts, and con artists.

   True   Sort of True   False

Now add up your total score.

If you scored 10–14 points: Yikes! What in the world are you doing contemplating online dating? If you are this skeptical of online dating, then log off right now. Your doubts and vacillation will prevent you from finding success. And remember, Scripture instructs us to act from faith, not doubt (see James 1:6-8). If you feel doubts or shame associated with online dating, then don't get involved. Maybe this book will help you process and rethink some of your doubts and questions, but I'm not out to change your mind. You need to examine your own attitudes and make your own decision.

If you scored 5–9 points: With this much doubt, are you sure you're ready? Your score indicates that you still have significant questions, and maybe some shame, about online dating. In general, most people initially do. Take another look at how you responded to the statements in the quiz. In which instances did you respond with True or Sort of True? Keep reading; the following chapters might clear up any lingering doubts. Also, pray about any doubts and questions you have. And don't begin dating on the Internet until you are confident before God that you are doing the right thing.

If you scored 0–4 points: You're almost ready to begin! Your score indicates that although you may have some minor doubts or questions, you are basically open to online dating. If you got your score because of one or two True responses, then make sure you read the rest of this book and pray about those feelings before you begin dating online. If those doubts don't go away and you aren't fully convinced that those statements are false, then online dating might not be for you. But keep an open mind and read on before making a final decision.

TIME TO GET STARTED

Contrary to some common assumptions about online dating, meeting others on the Internet does not mean you are socially inept or desperate. In fact, it's just the opposite. Christians who are successful in online dating have a high level of spiritual and emotional health. They also have a clear sense of who they are, what they believe, and what they are looking for in life. They begin the process with an objective assessment of themselves, becoming familiar with all they have to offer others, while also being aware of their weaknesses and areas of vulnerability.

Dating on the Internet also calls upon a person to be creative and articulate. Creativity helps your profile stand out from among the many uninspired and sometimes strange profiles. Skill in expressing yourself allows you to take advantage of the power of the written word to accurately present yourself and your beliefs, goals, and aspirations. These skills help you connect with like-minded Christians. Far from describing a loser, these skills are usually found in the type of person that other singles are most eager to meet!

In the chapters that follow, we will look at the knowledge, tools, and skills that increase a person's chances of finding his or her best match online. You will learn how to navigate the culture of cyberspace so you can develop safe and solid relationships. You will benefit from the wisdom of Scripture that will guide you as you seek God's direction and protection.

You will reach the same level of proficiency in the emotional, spiritual, and technical aspects of online relationship building rather than strengthening one area while neglecting other areas. And finally, you will find yourself growing spiritually and gaining greater self-understanding as you search for the love of your life.

Enough preliminaries. Let's get started!

Two

Look Inside Before You Log On

Know Yourself Before Making an Introduction

If you want to maximize your success in online dating, take time to prepare yourself before you log on. Be honest about what you're hoping to achieve, why you are drawn to meeting others online, and whether you have the emotional and spiritual foundations to be discerning and wise in the decisions you will need to make.

The best time to begin dating online is *after* you have examined your goals, motives, and expectations. You want to begin the process on the right foot so you won't end up learning lessons the hard way.

It's All in the Timing

Meeting and dating others online is a complicated process littered with questions and unexpected obstacles. It's best not to enter the territory unless your life is somewhat settled and you are on an even keel emotionally. Like every important endeavor, "there is a time for everything, and a season for every activity under heaven" (Ecclesiastes 3:1).

Ryan, a thirty-five-year-old divorced father of two young children, almost learned that lesson the hard way. "My divorce was devastating because of adultery on my wife's part," he says. "I was bitter and had to work through it. A year after the divorce, I thought I was ready to look again. But when I got online, I realized I was skeptical of everyone. I even met one woman in person, and although we seemed to click, I couldn't stop thinking that something must be wrong with her. Even worse, my personal life was hell. I was downsized and had to look for a new job. I had too much going on and was still too hurt from my divorce.

"But when I saw Samantha's online profile, I laughed at her humor. I sent her an e-mail, and it came back just as witty and normal as she had seemed in her profile. Since my life was so crazy, Samantha quickly became the bright spot in it. All of that was great, but I nearly blew it because I couldn't get enough of her. I would e-mail and instant-message her all the time. I wanted to meet her right away, but she wanted to go slow. When I recognized I was pushing her away, I backed off. And now I'm glad I did."

Ryan came close to blowing it with the woman who seems to be the answer to his prayers. Without intending to, he had become obsessive and pushy, which sent out a warning signal to Samantha. Because of the left-over unforgiveness and hurt from his divorce as well as the stress of adjusting to being an unemployed single parent, Ryan had too much chaos in his life to keep a clear mind for online dating. When he finally searched his heart, he realized he was looking for someone to calm his life down—an unrealistic expectation. He wisely decided to back off and let the relationship develop at its own pace. Today, he and Samantha are in a committed dating relationship.

Katrina, a registered nurse from San Jose, has never been married. She experienced ups and downs during three years of online dating, learning lessons along the way. Now she's in a committed relationship.

"I had been burned early on by thinking that the rush I felt…meant I had finally found my soul mate," she says. "In my mind I was ordering a bridal gown after just a couple of days of chatting with a certain man.

But after the high wore off, I had to admit we didn't have much in common. I ended up scaring off another person because I was so needy. I went through a similar process two more times before I decided to get some counseling. I didn't want to scare off every good man I met."

Dating online opened Katrina's eyes to her emotional neediness. Not everyone needs counseling to deal with past hurts, but Katrina's story does raise an important question: How do you know if you're ready for online dating?

Being ready means that you have the emotional health and stability, the skills, and the right outlook to be effective in developing relationships. To get a clearer picture of your spiritual and emotional readiness, take the following quiz. Circle the response that most closely describes your feelings and circumstances, then score 1 point for an Agree response and 0 points for a Disagree response.

1. I became single through a breakup, divorce, or death less than one year ago.

   Agree   Disagree

2. Most of the time I feel unattractive.

   Agree   Disagree

3. I'm lonely and feel depressed that I've been single for so long.

   Agree   Disagree

4. I seem to attract the wrong type of people, and I get hurt by those who seem to be attracted to me.

   Agree   Disagree

5. I struggle with addictions, codependency, and/or pornography.

   Agree   Disagree

6. Singleness feels more like a curse than a blessing.

   Agree   Disagree

7. Because I'm single, I feel as if a part of me is missing.

   Agree   Disagree

8. I'm not active in church or in a Christian ministry or outreach.

Agree   Disagree

9. I often feel that God is ignoring my prayers for a spouse.

Agree   Disagree

10. I don't feel confident that I can determine whether or not something is from God.

Agree   Disagree

Now add up your points.

If you scored 7–10: Back away from the computer, and no one will get hurt. Your score indicates that your timing is off. People who score in this range tend to become targets of those who use the Internet to take advantage of unsuspecting, needy, and naive people. A score in this range also puts you at risk for attracting people who aren't healthy enough or trustworthy enough to enter into a mature, godly relationship. Look over your responses in the quiz and pray about what you need to do to develop the emotional and spiritual maturity you need to succeed in online dating.

If you scored 4–6: Not too bad, but you're still not there. You have developed a degree of emotional and spiritual health that puts you on the right track. However, take a close look at the areas where you responded Agree, and examine your heart. Gaining a healthy, biblical perspective in these areas will help you find a good match. It takes self-confidence, interpersonal skills, and a strong and active expression of your faith to befriend and date Christians who are likely to enhance, not harm, your relationship with God.

If you scored 0–3: You're on your way. A score in this range reflects a high degree of self-confidence, emotional wellness, and spiritual vitality. You may have some areas in which you need to improve, but overall you should be experiencing success in your relationships both online and offline.

GET STARTED ON THE RIGHT FOOT

To get the best start in online dating, begin by looking inside. Are you feeling stressed out, lonely, or hurt by past relationships or a failed marriage? Your desire for companionship may feel overwhelming right now, but if the timing is not right, you could be setting yourself up for nothing but more hurt and rejection. Sometimes when people are facing big stressors in life, they give off vibes that can drive away the people who would actually be good for them. Or they send signals that they are vulnerable, attracting those who prey on emotionally needy people. If you jump in too soon, you're only hurting yourself.

The apostle Peter issued this warning:

> Humble yourselves, therefore, under God's mighty hand, that he may lift you up in due time. Cast all your anxiety on him because he cares for you. Be self-controlled and alert. Your enemy the devil prowls around like a roaring lion looking for someone to devour.
> (1 Peter 5:6-8)

Those who are burdened or weary may not be self-controlled or alert enough to watch for the schemes of the Enemy. So ask yourself if the timing is right for you to start or continue dating online. To help answer that question, review the list below and place a check mark next to the challenges you have faced this past year. Then answer the question that follows.

During the past twelve months, I have faced...
    ____ health problems
    ____ sexual or emotional infidelity
    ____ divorce
    ____ conflict with parents, siblings, and/or other family members

____ custody battles or other problems with my former spouse

____ social isolation or a change in social activities

____ family turmoil

____ problems with my job or coworkers

____ being fired or downsized

____ the death of a spouse, child, other family member, or close friend

____ problems with my children

____ gaining or losing a roommate or a live-in family member

____ moving to a new residence or city

____ problems with a landlord or neighbors

____ starting a new job or achieving major personal success

____ experiencing a major personal failure

____ health or behavior problems of a family member or close friend

____ loss of or damage to personal property

____ a vacation or trip

____ the loss of a friend or family member due to conflict or a move

____ financial difficulties

____ falling victim to abuse or violent crime

____ legal problems

How do you feel you have coped with the challenges you have experienced this past year? In what ways, if any, do you think these challenges have affected your readiness for online dating?

TAKE A LOOK INSIDE

The life events described in the quiz—even the good ones—produce stress. Too many of these events occurring close together can throw off your equilibrium and inhibit your ability to make grounded decisions. Further, the more stress there is in your life, the less able you will be to invest energy and emotion in your search for a new relationship.

For the events you marked Yes, pay close attention to how well you are coping. Do you notice a pattern, such as feeling overwhelmed, angry, fatigued, depressed, or lonely? All of these feelings are normal emotions and don't necessarily mean you aren't ready for online dating. However, your answers can reveal whether you have the time and energy available at this point to invest in such a demanding process.

Do you have time to check e-mail and write to ten or fifteen people a day? Do you have time to monitor and update your profile? Are you healed emotionally from your last relationship? If not, you're not yet ready to give another person a fair shot. Are your home life, work life, and friendships stable enough to share with another person? If not, you are likely to pull another person into the chaos that is unfolding around you.

Are you extremely lonely because of one or more of these life events? If so, do you feel that you need another person in your life to cure that loneliness? Are you feeling depressed as you mourn a loss, an illness, a death, or some other devastating event? If so, can you honestly say that you are ready to be emotionally available to another person?

Be honest with yourself as you think through your answers to these questions. Recognize that if you have a history of any type of addiction, if you have experienced a string of unhealthy relationships, or if you have struggled (or are struggling) with pornography, online dating might not be in your best interest at this time. Before you can enter into healthy online dating, you need to take the time to know yourself and deal with any problem areas in your life. Otherwise, you may end up hurting yourself or those you meet online, further damaging your chances of developing meaningful relationships. If you realize that the timing is not right, then do yourself a favor and wait until you're ready. The opportunities won't disappear just because you delayed dating online for a few months or a year.

WHY ARE YOU SINGLE?

Don't you just love this question? If you're tired of hearing it, then rest up. You'll have to answer it repeatedly online. Some of the most common questions asked in profiles at online dating sites are variations on these:

- Why are you still single?
- Have you ever been married or in a committed relationship?
- How did the relationship end and what did you learn?

You will regularly hear these questions asked by potential matches, and you need to have honest answers ready. Your answers also reflect how well you are coping with your broken relationships and where you are in the grieving process. Although you shouldn't reveal intimate details of your past relationships, most people want to know in general terms what happened to your most recent serious relationship. They are curious about whether you have accepted the breakup and have learned whatever lessons there are to learn. They want to know, as well, if you have healed from the depression, resentment, and anger. No one wants to date a person who is bitter, cynical, or still mourning the loss of an ex.

Think about your most recent dating relationship as you complete the following inventory.

    1. How long ago was the breakup or loss?

2. How important were the person and the relationship to you? Explain.

3. If your relationship ended in a breakup, what would the other person say caused the breakup? How would you describe the cause of the breakup?

4. If the relationship ended in death, how would you describe how well you are coping with the loss? Do you honestly believe that you could trust your heart to loving another person as deeply again?

After answering the above questions, review your responses and ask yourself the following questions. As you think about these four questions, pay close attention to any red flags that indicate you might not have healed enough from your last relationship to begin searching for a new one. You might want to seek input and perspective from a close friend or trusted family member. Ask that person to read over your responses so you can get an outside appraisal.

1. What is the overall tone of my responses? Do words such as *angry, bitter, resentful,* or *depressed* come to mind?

2. Am I blaming my ex for everything that went wrong in the relationship or for most of the problems that led to the relationship's failure? Explain.

3. What positive things, if any, came out of the relationship?

4. Do I have lingering anger or resentment toward my ex, myself, or God? Explain.

STAGES OF GRIEF

If you are still healing from a past relationship, check to see where you may be in the typical stages of the grieving process. As you read the following descriptions, determine whether you are stuck in any of the stages and need to seek God's healing before you pursue another relationship.

- *Denial:* "This isn't happening." In this stage, you refuse to accept that the other person is never coming back.

- *Anger/resentment:* "Why did you have to do this to me?" In this stage, your anger and resentment are expressed in statements that blame the other person, God, or others for the tremendous pain you are feeling.

- *Bargaining:* "What can I do to make things go back to the way they were?" Bargaining reflects your desire to do anything but accept the reality of the loss. (In fact, this stage can often precede the anger/resentment stage.) Those experiencing grief may negotiate with God in an attempt to bring the other person back. Those facing a breakup may negotiate with the other person, using a willingness to change as a bargaining chip to try to keep the relationship intact.

- *Depression:* "Why is this happening to me?" In this stage, anger and attempts at negotiating give way to profound sadness and even despair. Many feel as if they will never find love again. Some will beat themselves up over the mistakes they made, allowing self-judgment to spread into a general belief that they don't have what it takes to make a relationship work.

- *Acceptance:* "I'll be okay, and in time I'll be happy again." Once people reach this stage, they have mourned the loss and realize that they can move on with their lives. Feelings of depression or anger may occasionally resurface, but these feelings do not characterize the person's general emotional state.

Jeffrey, a customer service agent from Alabama, started dating online after his divorce. He didn't recognize the stages of grief at first, but gradually he began to realize what was happening as he interacted with online contacts.

"[My ex-wife] committed adultery and had no remorse," he says. "How do you forgive someone who doesn't even see that she needs forgiveness?

How are you supposed to talk about adultery [with anyone] and not sound upset? One woman I met [online] told me I sounded like I still had some unforgiveness in my heart that I needed to let go of. I guess I didn't want to deal with the truth."

Jeffrey brings up a good point: How do you talk about a painful breakup or loss without being real about your feelings? No one wants you to pretend that you are past the grief when you're not. So rather than fake it, take the time to understand what you are feeling about your last relationship. Understanding your own feelings as well as the stages of grief will help you constructively discuss that relationship with any serious matches you find online.

A Healthy Body Image

One of the most hotly debated issues in online singles communities is the role that physical appearance and attractiveness should play in dating. The issue of a person's weight, in particular, tends to elicit conflicting and even angry responses. Most agree that a person's character and spiritual maturity are far more important than his or her outward appearance (see 1 Samuel 16:7). However, physical attractiveness does play a role in the chemistry between two people. So how can we balance the two, giving primary consideration to a person's character without denying the reality of physical attraction?

Most Web sites for singles, including Christian-oriented sites, require that you include some description of your body dimensions in your personal profile. Frequently there is a height and weight disclosure as well as a general description of your body proportions and muscle tone, such as "average-toned," "athletic," "a few extra pounds," or "big and beautiful."

Differences in how people prioritize physical appearance surface regularly. Men tend to spell out their preferences in their online posts, while women rarely make an issue of height or weight requirements. A common complaint from those who are overweight or feel they are unattractive is that others judge them based on their looks without first getting to know their heart.

One of the most popular matchmaking sites, *eharmony.com*, addresses this concern by describing its online dating process as "falling in love from the inside out." Subscribers to this service were initially allowed to look at pictures of a match only after they had corresponded through a structured process of guided communication in which matches were encouraged to focus on the other person's character and inner beauty. However, *eharmony.com* later acknowledged that men in particular were reluctant to fall in love without having a clear idea of what the other person looked like. As a result, the site has allowed pictures to be exchanged at any point in the relationship-building process.[1]

"Is preferring certain attributes for the person you plan to spend the rest of your life with judging [that person], or is it simply making a decision about your life?" asks John, a stockbroker from New York who has been dating online for two years. "Just because I prefer something doesn't mean I hate anyone who does not fit that description. It only seems to come up when you talk about a person's weight. But no one questions your Christianity when you say you prefer a person of a certain age or a person with or without kids."

It's not surprising that women who date online see the issue differently: "I often feel upset about the looks obsession," says Stacey, an office manager from Denver. "Even my mom says things like 'If you lose a little bit of weight, then guys might look at you more.' It's discouraging because I feel that I am physically attractive and have an engaging personality. I don't think even the Christian guys can look past extra pounds. They couch their stuff by saying their match will need to take care of her body like it's the temple of the Holy Spirit. Or they'll say the match must be height and weight proportionate. Is that a buzzword for 'skinny'? I don't answer profiles that mention body issues. And if a guy asks for a picture too soon, I just end it right there."

Most people are not entirely satisfied with their appearance. That's normal. But Stacey and others who share her view could actually be pulling the plug on relationships that might otherwise blossom. They don't give a match who asks for a photo any chance to develop the relationship further.

WHAT'S "AVERAGE"?

When you include a physical description in your personal profile, it's important to be current and accurate without going into too much detail. I see many profiles where people describe their size or body proportions as "average." This may accurately reflect the person's self-perception, but it can put off matches who have a different understanding of what *average* means—or even what *overweight* means.

In part, this is a cultural issue. Some cultures have a standard of beauty that elevates women with curves. In addition, many of us may be accustomed to a body type based on family history and experience in which a full-figured female shape may seem normal rather than overweight. A person from this particular culture or family background might tend to shy away from a potential match who is considered too thin.

Aside from the influence of background, people tend to judge weight differently. Many women may correctly consider themselves average because the typical dress size for American women ranges from 12 to 18, not the tiny sizes that Hollywood portrays as the desirable norm. So to avoid confusion over whether someone's body proportions fit a match's preferences, many online daters simply request a recent picture.

If you have concerns about sending a photo too early in the process, it's best to get that part over with before you invest too much emotion in an online relationship. Sure, the person could fall in love with your heart without seeing a picture. But he or she may struggle later with the way you look. Why live in fear of rejection? No relationship can grow if you are constructing emotional walls to protect yourself from possible rejection.

All of us have preferences and turnoffs. One person seeks a match who is thin, while the next person wants curves, and yet another person seeks intelligence and a sense of humor without regard to weight issues. Most of the time people think their weight, height, or body type causes them to be unfairly rejected. But often that has nothing to do with it. A person's character and personality can be powerfully attractive or a major turnoff. In any event, if you have to reject a potential match, make sure you discuss your preferences in Christian love. And never give the person false hope after you have determined the match is just not right.

Take a Fresh Look at Loneliness

Although millions of Christians are trying to find their soul mates online, not all of these Christians are spiritually or emotionally healthy. Some Christians feel that being single is a curse, so they put their lives on hold until they get married. Scan the profiles, and you'll see headlines such as "Lonely Christian in search of…" The person feels incomplete and is waiting for the blessing of a spouse so life can really begin. This is a big red flag, a warning that shouts: "I'm a needy, dependent person. Steer clear!"

Loneliness is not wrong or sinful. Adam felt lonely before sin ever entered the picture, and God provided human companionship to address

Adam's loneliness. In that instance, the companion was a spouse, but friends and family members also help meet our need for companionship. Many Christians think that just because they are lonely, God will give them a mate. But God doesn't promise each one of us a mate. So don't conclude that your life is meaningless unless you're married. And if you're dating online, broaden your definition of success. You can find success by interacting with matches, learning more about yourself, and refining what you want and need in a spouse. Seeing your life as meaningful and defining success more broadly than merely getting married will help prevent you from burning out, getting hurt, or attracting the wrong people when you date online.

Brooke, a twenty-seven-year-old graduate student in New Jersey, learned this lesson the hard way. "My profile just reeked of loneliness and desperation," she admits, "and I attracted all sorts of weirdos. It was my wake-up call to do something about my life while I was still unattached to anyone."

If you struggle with loneliness, make sure you are actively doing things to counteract the negative side of this emotion. Combat it through prayer and regular involvement in the lives of others.

CAUSES OF LONELINESS

All of us—even married people—get lonely. But don't define yourself by that emotional state. (Read Galatians 5:22-23 for the characteristics that others should see in our lives.) Some of the negative attitudes associated with loneliness rob a person of joy and purpose. When that happens, you can become bitter and insecure, which will drive others away.

God has given us everything we need in Christ Jesus, so let's dig deeper into the spiritual questions—the soul cries—that may be fueling loneliness. If these issues are not addressed, they will undermine your search for a spouse. The first step is understanding your value in Christ: You are more significant to God than anything else in His creation. If you do not recognize your worth in God's eyes, you will place too much emphasis on how others respond to you. You will burden the other person in a relationship with the responsibility to prop up your sagging self-worth.

People are not attracted to those who identify themselves as being lonely. Instead, they are attracted to vibrant, positive, healthy people. According to Galatians 5:22, joy and patience are part of the fruit of the Spirit. Many Christians go online, post profiles, and send e-mails that are anything but joyful or patient. This type of behavior will drive healthy Christians away.

INTERNET ADDICTION

Online dating requires you to spend hours and hours at your computer. Some people, after having this much exposure to the Internet, find that they can't control how much time they spend online. If computer and online usage begins to cause serious disruptions in a person's life, he or she may have an Internet addiction.

People who struggle with addictions—particularly pornography—and those who have been wounded by a series of unhealthy relationships might find they should avoid online dating. Ask yourself if the costs of being online outweigh the benefits.

Addiction can be defined as a dependence on a substance, a person, or a behavior that harms you physically, emotionally, socially, or spiritually. A person who has an addiction is not able to stop the behavior without experiencing unpleasant withdrawal symptoms. If you question whether you are addicted to a substance, a relationship, or an activity (including surfing the Internet), consult with a qualified psychologist or therapist.

The following questions will help you determine if the Internet might

feed any tendencies you have toward addictive behaviors. Answering Yes
to any of these questions means that you need to determine if you are
healthy enough to develop and maintain positive relationships online.

*Are you involved in or do you have a history of engaging in any of the follow-
ing behaviors?*

1. Taking a substance or being involved in an activity or relationship where you find yourself powerless to stop or walk away.
   Yes   No

2. Taking a substance or being involved in an activity or relationship where you have experienced or are experiencing harmful or
   destructive consequences in your social, occupational, physical,
   emotional, or spiritual life.
   Yes   No

3. Taking a substance or being involved in an activity or relationship that is producing or has produced chaotic or unmanage-
   able consequences in your life.
   Yes   No

4. Taking a substance or being involved in an activity or relationship where you have to take or seek more of the substance,
   activity, or relationship just to get the same pleasurable feelings
   you once had.
   Yes   No

5. Finding yourself going through withdrawal symptoms when
   you try to quit taking a substance or when you try to end your
   involvement in an activity or relationship.
   Yes   No

If your response to any of these statements was Yes, ask yourself if
you are strong enough to resist the temptations that will come, uninvited,

from certain Web sites, unsolicited e-mails, and Internet pornographers. This can serve as a wake-up call for you to seek help if you need it or for you to help a friend who has become addicted to the Internet.

YOUR SPIRITUAL HEALTH

It's important to assess your own spiritual health before you begin dating online. Your potential matches will be interested in your commitments as a Christian and what you are doing to keep your spiritual life vital. Remember that when you date online it's acceptable and even expected to ask no-nonsense questions about most areas of a person's life. For Christian singles, no other area receives more attention than faith and spirituality. So think about how you put your faith into action.

Although 1 Peter 3:15 tells us to always be prepared to give our testimonies, many of us are unable to do so. When you are online, you will have the opportunity to share your faith story with many people. What will you say about your spiritual life and beliefs?

Another reason for assessing your spiritual health is to identify areas that need improvement so you can find your identity in Christ rather than seeking affirmation in the praise or admiration of others. To help you assess your spiritual health, answer the following questions. Then review your answers and ask God to open your eyes to areas in your relationship with Him in which you need greater depth, growth, and maturity.

1. When did you become a Christian? Why did you decide to follow Christ?

2. What are your talents and spiritual gifts, and how have you used them for the glory of God?

3. What ministries are you involved in now and why? In what other capacities, if any, do you long to serve?

4. How would you describe your church? Why did you choose to become a member there? What keeps you there?

5. Describe how close you feel to God right now. In what ways have you grown in your relationship with Him? In what areas do you need to grow more?

6. If you could ask God any questions about things that make you angry, sad, or frustrated, what would you ask Him?

7. How important is prayer in your life? When was the last time you prayed (other than saying a blessing at mealtime)? What did you pray for?

8. How do you think God is leading your life?

9. What dreams do you have for your life? Do you believe God will turn these dreams into reality? Why or why not?

10. What are the issues that cause you to doubt God? In what areas of your life are you doubting Him now?

11. How many older or more mature Christians are you regularly in contact with? How many do you consider mentors?

12. How many close Christian friends do you have? Do you feel a sense of family when you go to church or are around other Christians? Why or why not?

The psalmist calls us not only to obey God and serve Him but to find our delight in Him:

Delight yourself in the LORD and he will give you the desires of your heart. Commit your way to the LORD; trust in him and he will do this: He will make your righteousness shine like the dawn, the justice of your cause like the noonday sun. Be still before the LORD and wait patiently for him. (Psalm 37:4-7)

As you assess your spiritual health and your level of trust in God, consider the following:

- Although singleness may involve periods of loneliness, it is a time of blessing and a stage of life in which you can devote undivided attention to God.
- Marriage is created by God and receives His blessing. But marriage will never complete you as a person. You are already complete in Christ.
- By studying God's Word, you can develop the discernment to know what is from God and what is from the Enemy.

Jessica, a waitress from Boston, has been dating online for eight months. She experienced firsthand that meeting Christians online means you'll encounter a wide range of approaches to the Christian faith: "When I first went online, I met the most wonderful Christian man who was everything I wanted," she says. "There was one problem though. He was down on anything that had to do with church or organized religion. He had been burned by hypocrites in a couple of churches. I knew that all he needed was to be around the loving Christians at my church and he would be back. But I learned the hard way that I can't fix anyone. We were together for more than six months after meeting offline, and I just couldn't get him to get past his hurt…. After so many months of spiritual sacrifice for the relationship, I had to end the relationship because it was messing up my own walk with God."

Each of us has a definition of what a Christian with an active faith looks like. Can you describe how you put your faith into action? Many women complain that too many men want a "good Christian woman" to help them stay on the straight and narrow. Given that God designed men to be the spiritual heads of their families, this lazy attitude couldn't be more wrong (see Ephesians 5:22-33). If you are a lukewarm Christian, that is exactly the kind of person you will attract. Want someone more mature? Then *you* have to become more mature.

Taking Your Faith Online

Discernment and wisdom are the spiritual gifts Christians typically want to have when they go online. These gifts will protect your heart as well as the hearts of those you meet online. By keeping your prayer life strong, you will become sensitive to the leading of the Holy Spirit to show you whether or not someone is a child of God. You'll also need the Holy Spirit to help you relate to others you will meet.

Tyler, a divorced store manager from Seattle, is engaged to someone he met online. But he recalls the early days when he was a newbie to online dating. "My ex-wife broke my heart when she left me for another man," he begins. "After twenty years of marriage, I did not know how to start over again. All my adult life I had been in only one major relationship. I felt stupid getting on the Internet. How would I know if this woman I was talking to was for real and wasn't just trying to use me? I prayed while I was reading profiles and making contact with women. It was a simple prayer that God would protect and keep me. I just wanted a real Christian woman—someone I could trust."

As you introduce yourself to others online, be confident in who you are as God's child. Ephesians 2:10 proclaims, "For we are God's workmanship, created in Christ Jesus to do good works." Do you believe that you are God's workmanship? This is the same God who created the majestic beauty of the heavens and the earth. Your own words and feelings about yourself and your relationship with God will tell you how deeply you believe these spiritual truths.

If you are serious about attracting the person God might approve as your mate, then you need to broadcast aspects about your faith in your profile and personal essays. When you are e-mailing or chatting with a match you find online, be prepared to answer the most common spiritual questions, such as When/how did you become a Christian? What denomination/church do you belong to? What do you believe about...? What is your relationship with God/Jesus like? How does it affect your daily life? If you find yourself struggling to answer any of these questions, discuss them with your minister or a trusted, spiritually mature friend or mentor.

As you approach online dating, remember that you are already complete in Christ. Be assured of your value as God's beautiful workmanship, and present yourself online as a confident, secure child of God.

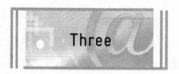

Check Your Goals
and Motivations

Make Sure You Know What You're Looking For

W hen you think about your life, what images come to mind? What are your private thoughts about your strongest longings and most important dreams? What gives your life purpose and meaning? What direction is your life taking? When people ask about your life, what do you tell them?

These are not easy questions to answer. We all seek meaning and purpose, and we all have hopes and dreams. But for many of us, the things we desire most seem to elude us.

A QUESTION OF CONTENTMENT

Most singles who attend church have heard sermons and Bible lessons on the need to be content in our singleness. That dreaded word—*contentment*—can elicit loud groans and energetic complaints. "It's easy for *you* to tell me to be content. You're going home to your husband [or wife] after this church service is over!"

We may also recall Paul's letter to the Christians at Corinth where he made the case that singleness is superior to marriage because singles can live in "undivided devotion to the Lord" (1 Corinthians 7:32-35). Today it would be a tough sell to convince many never-married singles and those who are single again that they should feel superior because they do not have a life partner. Notice that Paul was not saying that the desire to marry is a sin. Instead, he was drawing a comparison and reflecting an attitude that many churches today seem to ignore. Churches tend to emphasize families and provide support for married people, but they often fail to convey a strong, consistent message regarding the advantages of singleness. Paul, instead of looking at singleness as a second-class or interim stage of life, presented it as an honorable, desirable state. His attitude contradicts those who keep asking when you're going to get married, as if something is wrong with you.

The older I become, the more I like being able to do whatever I want without having to check with anyone. Am I 100 percent content with remaining single? No, but I do admit that being single has some perks. So without getting bogged down over the issue of contentment, let's focus instead on how we're spending the time God has given us while we're single. Do our activities reflect our devotion to God? Are we using our freedom as singles to live a vibrant life devoted to pleasing God?

These questions aren't intended as a guilt trip, but as a way to explore how faithfully you are living as a single Christian. Your answers to these questions make you interesting and attractive to other Christians. If you have no interests or commitments in life apart from searching for a mate, then you're not interesting to others. If you don't have clear goals and dreams in life or if you lack the desire to keep growing, changing, and learning, then you will come across as someone who is stuck in a boring rut. People want to know that your life counts for something and that you love God with more than just words.

Now for the flip side. If you are on fire for the Lord, I'd be the last person to tell you to keep it a secret. But in your online profile as well as in e-mails and chats, back off the Christianese. Religious jargon can come across as insincere, preachy, and, well, fake. I sense some of you bristling at this. You're asking, "Why should I dumb down the expression of my faith just to snag a date?" Believe me, I would never recommend such an approach. I'm just saying that coming across as "showy" or "preachy" may cause others to question your sincerity. Many Christian singles who date online complain that people who are showy or preachy tend to be the ones laying it on thick about their spiritual lives to hide insecurities or struggles that come to light later in the relationship.

Most Christian singles are just looking for a regular Christian, not a "superbeliever" who never has doubts or problems. Definitely express your faith, but make sure it's an honest, sincere, and genuine representation of the real you—normal human shortcomings and all—and not just the ideal you.

As you describe your life of faith, also keep in mind that online daters are looking for interesting people. If you have a ministry or a hobby that you really love, talk about it. Not everyone will find it fascinating, but some will. Just remember that you don't have to defend what you find interesting. If you dream of making your living as an artist, or moving to a city and teaching inner-city children, or just curling up on the sofa to watch a four-hour epic while sipping hot chocolate, then so be it. Don't be ashamed of your interests or dreams just because those who prefer opera may not understand them.

What's Your Objective?

The goal of online dating is to widen your search at the same time you are narrowing the field based on areas of shared interest and life compatibility. The Internet enables you to conduct such a search with unprecedented speed and efficiency. When you meet someone at church or at a party, you will never by the end of the evening be able to gather all the information about his or her interests, goals, pet peeves, and desires that you can find with the click of a mouse while looking at online profiles. If you tried to do this in person, you'd come across like a cop grilling a suspect. When talking face to face, people don't like to get that personal that quickly. But with online dating, you can post your dreams and find out who else might share those dreams.

Steven, a man in his thirties who met his fiancée, Tiffany, online, was bold enough to put his dreams on the Internet. "When I read his profile," Tiffany says, "he talked about being a business executive who had decided his life was going in the wrong direction. He said he became a Christian, and then all of a sudden his MBA didn't matter as much. He just wanted to be happy in what he did, and his ministry of counseling at-risk youth made him happier than the money he made at work. So one day he quit and went back to school to get a counseling degree. Sure, at first I thought this could be someone who didn't know what he wanted to be when he grew up. But when I talked to him, he was so passionate about his work with kids. I found that so attractive."

Each of us has a life (or we should have one), but many of us never make the effort to give our life the careful thought and consideration it deserves. So before you post your profile, set aside time to identify what abilities or qualities you can share with others. In fact, do this *before* you make a list of the qualities you're seeking in a match. What do you have to offer someone else? Instead of thinking of life starting when you get married, make sure you *already have* a life to share with someone else. The following questions will help you discover and describe your life.

1. What are your top three goals in life?

2. What are you most passionate about? Why are you so emotionally connected to the object of your passion?

3. Where do you see your life heading in the next three years?

4. What do you *not* like about your life? What steps are you taking to change those things?

5. What three activities do you most enjoy doing when you're not
   at work? (For example, volunteer or service activities, ministries,
   community involvement, etc.)

6. What are the top three things you do just for fun?

7. What are your favorite books, movies, and styles of music?

8. How often do you travel? Where was the last place you visited that you really enjoyed? Where would you like to visit next?

9. Do you think God is pleased with how you spend your free time? Why or why not?

10. What three things would make you happier—apart from finding your perfect match?

Answering these questions should help you see yourself and your life more clearly, and it will give you important clues about the type of person you want to share your life with.

With that work done, it's time to take a closer look at your expectations and motivations as you approach online dating. You need to do this both for yourself and for those you will date online. No one likes to deal with a person who has a hidden agenda. And it's even worse when a person's agenda is hidden from himself or herself.

The psalmist prayed, "Search me, O God, and know my heart; test me and know my anxious thoughts. See if there is any offensive way in me, and lead me in the way everlasting" (Psalm 139:23-24). A good place to start is to ask yourself, and God, why meeting others online appeals to you. Ask God to help you examine and test your motivations and expectations, and ask him to reveal any hidden agendas or impure motives. You need this understanding before you post a profile. Most of your reasons will reflect the motivations that most online daters share in common. But some of your motivations may reveal expectations and hopes that are inappropriate or simply impossible to fill.

MEET YOUR MOTIVATIONS

Many people, while dating online, discover motivations they are surprised they have. Typically, online daters discover their hidden motivations when they try to troubleshoot why their search is stalled or why their online relationships fail. Sometimes motivations are revealed through prayer and the prompting of the Holy Spirit. The typical reasons people try online dating are (1) to have more options, (2) to date with convenience and privacy, and (3) to have greater ease in gauging compatibility with another person. Sometimes, however, online daters discover they have other motivations.

"After I got divorced," Monica says, "I went online out of curiosity. I had gained some weight but was working out, so I posted a picture of myself before the weight gain and I got many responses. In my marriage I felt unattractive. But online I found many good men wanting to be with me. I began to feel so good about myself and worked out harder just in case one of those relationships turned out to be something.

"After I lost the weight, I started to notice the attention I was getting offline. I met someone at church and began dating, so I stopped talking to the men I had met online. One day I got online, and one man instant-messaged me and asked me why I had disappeared. He thought we were moving toward something. I told him I met someone from church whom I wanted to pursue. He asked if I had been playing some sort of game. When he sent me an article about how people hurt others online, I had to admit that I saw myself. I really only used those good Christian men as a motivation for losing weight and to boost my self-esteem. God was busting me."

Monica's story shows how easy it is to get distracted by the attention and self-confidence boost that can come through online dating. Innocent people can be hurt by someone who hasn't thought through his or her motivations before getting online.

QUESTION YOUR MOTIVATIONS

To help you think through your own motivations, honestly ask yourself if any of the following statements match how you feel.

"I've had limited experience in dating, and the thought of gaining a lot of experience with so many people intrigues me."

Some people who may not have had much experience in romantic situations see online dating as a way to practice for the "real thing" or even as a way to make up for lost time. In offline social networks, most singles have never had fifteen different people vying for their attention. Dating online can make most people more popular than they ever felt in offline social settings. If your main motivation is to feel popular, you will create havoc in the lives of marriage-minded Christians because you will probably resist becoming exclusive with someone.

> *"When I meet an interesting person online, I'm in no hurry to meet that person face to face. Even if I feel we are growing closer, I'm still okay with keeping things online."*

If you prefer to continue communicating online even when you have developed strong feelings for a person, then ask yourself if your motive for being online is really to seek a serious, long-term relationship. Or do you crave the romance and excitement of falling in love rather than being willing to develop an actual relationship? Are you put off by the risks and challenges involved in developing an in-person relationship? If so, are you trying to mask feelings of inadequacy or insecurity? No matter what motivates you, it's dishonest to allow others to think you're interested in a serious relationship that will eventually move offline if you're really not.

> *"After my breakup, I went online to pass the time. I was lonely and wanted to meet people just to talk. I guess I'd prefer to meet people face to face since I have doubts about the people I meet online."*

If this comes close to describing your feelings, your motive for going online may be to pass time while you heal from a broken relationship. You are not seeking a relationship but are feeding off the attention you get online to help boost your confidence or patch up a damaged ego after a breakup. The problem with this motive is obvious: It's selfish, or at the very least, it shows that you are oblivious to the feelings of others. When you talk with someone every day without having any desire to move the relationship offline, you will only end up causing pain for the other person.

"I find that I don't know what to do or say around members of the opposite sex. Dating online allows me the opportunity to learn."

If your goal is to meet as many people online as possible so you can practice your social skills and develop friendships, then shift your thinking away from online dating and instead spend time in online singles communities, such as message boards or Christian chat rooms. An online community for Christian singles is great for fellowship, for asking questions and floating ideas, for sharing observations and insights, and for prayer requests. Online communities give you a chance to fellowship with a wide variety of believers without the expectation that you are seeking to develop a dating relationship.

"In several instances I have met someone online, and we seemed to click. But when we move the relationship offline, it never works out. The relationship always seems better when it remains online."

If your offline meetings or relationships don't work, or if the person tells you in person that you are not what he or she expected, you might be using online dating to project an ideal self—the person you wish you were. When you communicate online, you might come across as wittier, more sensitive, more eloquent, or more caring than you are in person. And many times you might not be aware of how much of a discrepancy there is between your online self and your actual self. Here's a rule of thumb: The wider the gap between your online self and your offline self, the more likely it will be that a relationship won't survive when it leaves the anonymity and social distance of cyberspace.

One or more of the above motivations may fit your situation, or you may feel that none of them describes you. The point of answering these questions is to help you examine your own behavior and reactions in order to identify a deeper motive. For the sake of the people you meet online, be clear about your own motivations.

CHECK YOUR EXPECTATIONS

Most online dating experts and successful daters agree that it's best to keep your expectations low. I'm not suggesting that you project a negative image or that you be fatalistic about the process. Instead, realize that despite the advertisements highlighting couples who found each other online, there are many more failures than fairy-tale marriages.

When you date online, you can control only one person: yourself. You can't control the reactions of others. On television and on the Internet, you will see scores of happy couples who were brought together through an online dating service for "an investment of as little as nineteen dollars a month." You won't see commercials featuring the 75 percent of online relationships that never make it to an in-person date. Most dating sites are tight-lipped about their success rates. It has been speculated that less than 1 percent of online dating relationships progress all the way to marriage.[1] Some sites with higher success rates, such as Christian dating sites, increase a person's chances for success by being more selective in whom they accept for membership. By focusing on a more homogenous niche market, they increase the rate of success.

But why do online dating services have such low success rates overall? Part of the reason is that online dating is a very recent phenomenon. The number of Christians online is still growing and is limited in some demographic groups, such as ethnic minorities. As the stigma surrounding online dating subsides in the Christian community, greater numbers of spiritually healthy singles will become involved, and this will increase the numbers of serious, marriage-minded singles from whom to choose. Success rates also are influenced by the scores of individuals who crash and burn due to heartbreak or disappointment caused by unrealistic expectations, spiritual and emotional unhealthiness, or inadequate relationship-building skills. Again, the right preparation will greatly improve your chances for success.

To move ahead in your own preparation, respond to the following statements about your expectations for your time and efforts online. Circle either Agree or Disagree to determine which of these statements reflect your own beliefs.

1. To find a spouse, all I need to do is increase the number of singles I interact with online.

    Agree   Disagree

2. Surely I can find my spouse among the millions of people with profiles on the Internet. It would be almost impossible *not* to.

    Agree   Disagree

3. When I get going with online dating, I know I'll have a full inbox of e-mails from interested Christian singles.

    Agree   Disagree

4. Online dating is so much better—and easier—than trying to meet like-minded singles the traditional way. I know this is the solution for my previous failures and frustrations.

    Agree   Disagree

5. Online dating is so convenient that it will allow me to squeeze a social life into my packed schedule.

    Agree   Disagree

6. What do I have to lose? If a match doesn't work out, at least I won't have to see the other person's expression when I announce that it's over.

    Agree   Disagree

7. Online dating will solve the problems that always used to crop up in my dating life.

Agree   Disagree

8. Once a "true" Christian falls in love with my heart, there is no way things like my physical appearance will get in the way.

Agree   Disagree

If you hold any of these expectations, they will lead to frustration, hurt, and burnout. Online dating is not the cure for loneliness or the solution for everything that has gone wrong in your past dating relationships. It is not a guarantee that you will find a mate. It is simply a tool to aid your search. Placing too much importance on online dating will set you up for disappointment.

ARE YOU *REALLY* READY?

Now that you have examined your heart, your goals, your motivations, and your expectations—inviting God to open your eyes so you'll recognize any blind spots—you are better prepared for the challenges you will encounter online. Online dating requires verbal skills and computer skills, creativity, confidence, and spiritual and emotional health. You may send hundreds of e-mails and receive only a 5 percent response. If you are not prepared, a simple thing like a low response rate can cause you to lose confidence.

Success in online dating requires you to "trust in the LORD and do good" (Psalm 37:3) so that the joy of the Lord will radiate through you, even in your profile and your e-mails. And you must rest in the promise that if you actively delight in God, He "will give you the desires of your heart" (Psalm 37:4). The outcome is up to God, so trust Him to work. And wait patiently for His blessings.

If you are ready to begin, pray the following prayer—or one of your own—asking God for traveling mercies before you go online.

Heavenly Father, I know you created me with a plan and purpose for my life. Please help me draw close to you and delight myself in you. Help me commit my life to serve others so that all may see how much I love you. Please, dear Lord, help me remain focused on you and not on a search for love and romance. Help me strengthen any areas that you have revealed as weaknesses in which Satan can attack me. Protect me from hurting someone else or becoming the victim of evil.

Lord, I give this search over to you and pray that you will guide my steps. If you do not approve of any of my choices, please give me the wisdom to accept a no from you as being in my best interest. Lord, please bless the other people who are seeking spouses online. Especially comfort those who might be confused if I choose not to continue toward a deeper relationship. Please grant them the desires of their hearts. I pray that all my choices online will be made to your glory. In Jesus's name. Amen.

Four

Rules of the Cyber-Road

Internet Skills That Increase Your Success Rate

W hen you were a teenager in driver's training, part of the learning process was recognizing and decoding road signs. Some are warning signs (Construction Ahead or Narrow Bridge), some are regulatory (vehicle weight or height limits), some are restrictive (speed limits or no-passing zones), and some are merely informational (gas, food, lodging). Understanding the purpose of a road sign helps you read it accurately and gain the most benefit from it. It also increases your chances for a safe and enjoyable road trip.

Likewise, as you travel in cyberspace, you need to read the signs along the way. Just as a new driver learns the meaning and purpose of road signs, so a traveler in cyberspace gets around more quickly if he or she knows how to read the signs. This includes having a degree of technical skill, knowing the lingo and terminology, and understanding the symbolic representations of feeling, emotion, and "tone of voice," called *emoticons*. In chapter 2 we began the process of assessing your spiritual and emotional readiness to begin dating online. In this chapter we will examine the final three areas that will make you more effective in your online search.

The rules of the road for online dating include cyberstyle, cybersecurity, and Netspeak—unique ways to communicate online. Each skill contributes to greater success and enjoyment in online dating. After mastering these skills, you will attract the type of people who, like you, are looking for a healthy, godly marriage.

The following quiz will help you assess your familiarity with the Internet and your ability to use the Web for online dating.

Cyberstyle

1. I don't know where to find online communities where I can interact with like-minded Christians.

    Agree   Disagree

2. I have never before met or befriended people online.

    Agree   Disagree

3. I often feel left out of online groups or communities, and I don't know why.

    Agree   Disagree

4. I don't know how to determine if someone online is truly a Christian.

    Agree   Disagree

5. I don't understand the differences between building relationships online and doing it in person.

    Agree   Disagree

Cybersecurity

1. People often tell me that I'm too trusting of others.

    Agree   Disagree

2. I am sometimes hurt or taken advantage of by others.

    Agree   Disagree

3. I do not know all the ways to protect myself while meeting new people online.

   Agree   Disagree

4. I do not know the warning signs that tell me someone I've met online is abusive or is otherwise untrustworthy or simply not right for me.

   Agree   Disagree

5. I am not confident about my ability to know how to safely and effectively move an online relationship to an in-person meeting.

   Agree   Disagree

Netspeak

1. I do not know the most common acronyms people use on the Internet during e-mail conversations, chats, instant messaging, and on message boards.

   Agree   Disagree

2. I am not sure I know how to effectively convey emotions in my online conversations.

   Agree   Disagree

3. People have told me that I have trouble expressing myself verbally and/or in writing.

   Agree   Disagree

4. I do not know what types of issues and topics are best left to in-person, rather than online, conversations.

   Agree   Disagree

5. I do not know the signs that indicate when people are telling the truth both online and offline.

   Agree   Disagree

Now add up the total number of Agree responses in all three sections.

If you scored 9–15: You are way too vulnerable to go online right now! Your score indicates that you are not prepared to safely navigate the Internet. You need to develop skills so you can protect yourself against the evil and unhealthy people in cyberspace. You also need to develop some offensive skills—things you do well—so you can stand out among the millions who are online. Look back over your answers and see which area or areas of cybernavigation you need to explore in more depth.

If you scored 5–8: Proceed carefully—you might be heading for an accident! Your responses indicate that you are familiar with some but not all of the necessary aspects of cybertravel. Just one mistake can cause a huge wreck online. Check your answers to see which areas need the most attention.

If you scored 0–4: You are ready to go, but remain vigilant. If your score is zero, then you are truly ready to dive in. But if you scored one to four, beef up the areas where you are weak, and then move forward. It takes just one mistake to hurt yourself or others.

Even if you scored well on the quiz, don't overestimate your knowledge. Make sure you truly have all the skills you need for journeying in cyberspace. People tend to believe that it's only "other people" who fall into online traps. The information and principles in this chapter are designed to give you the basic information you need to travel safely.

A Travel Guide to Cyberstyle

Cyberstyle refers to an understanding of the way things work online and the ability to use this knowledge to seek out and build strong online relationships. Merely posting an ad won't yield the results you want unless you have a fundamental understanding of the rules of style that are unique to cyberspace. For instance, knowing where to post your profile is just as important as knowing what to say in it. Understanding how online relationships develop is critically important to your success in online dating.

And it's important to know that online communities have their own culture—their own rules and protocol for what is appropriate to say, how to say it, and how to interact with others. If you don't know the rules, you can drive people away.

With an understanding of the types of Internet singles sites, you can evaluate them to determine if they will yield interactions with the type of Christian singles you are most interested in. You will also understand how to relate to others and know the benefits and limitations of online relationship building. (In chapter 5 you will find an in-depth discussion of the different types of singles sites.)

There are five basic places Christians meet other singles online:

- *Matchmaker sites*—These sites use objective criteria as well as data on personal preferences, your personality, and other unique characteristics to screen potential matches before sending you the most compatible matches for consideration.
- *Online ad sites*—These sites give searchers the freedom to screen profiles on their own and decide for themselves whom they want to pursue. Online ad sites make up the biggest category of dating sites and have large numbers of members.
- *Chat rooms*—These are interactive forums, organized by topic, where up to fifty people can chat with one another in real time. (Generally not recommended for dating purposes.)
- *Message boards*—These online forums or groups are organized by topic or demographic group. Members engage in ongoing discussions by "posting" a message that remains available on the message board for a period of time. Singles can sometimes meet prospective dates when they notice posts from like-minded people.
- *Internet game sites*—On these sites people meet to play online games such as chess or bingo. Many of these sites have chat rooms where people can chat with others while engaging in a game. Though not

intended for dating purposes, people can often strike up friendships while playing games, which can sometimes develop into more.

Finding the Best Web Sites

Since online dating is still growing, especially in the Christian market, Web sites tend to come and go. To find those sites currently in operation, do a search in any search engine (such as Google or Yahoo!) for "Christian single" or "Christian dating," and the top sites should pop up. Keep in mind that not all sites that show up in the results will be Christian sites run for and/or by Christians. For example, *eharmony.com* is featured in Christian media and has a Christian founder, but its services are available both to Christians and non-Christians. Other sites are run by secular companies but desire to attract Christian singles. The largest sites are secular.

This is not intended to imply that there is anything wrong with searching on secular sites. This information is provided only so you won't assume that all the sites that show up in a search for Christian dating are Christian. Furthermore, matchmaker sites may be open to all types of people, but they will not send you non-Christian matches if you indicate an exclusive preference for Christians. And since site members are prevented from searching profiles on their own, you won't receive e-mails from non-Christian members. This is not the case for online ad sites, however. Although you may limit your search to those who identify themselves as Christians, anyone can send you an e-mail.

One of the most important and useful skills you can possess is the ability to evaluate Web sites to determine if they are worth your time and money. Ask yourself, With everything going on at this site and the composition of the membership, are there so many ungodly distractions that it will be difficult for me to hear God's voice? Many Christians leave secular sites because they receive too many inappropriate e-mails. The best way to choose appropriate sites is to follow these basic rules:

- Know who runs the site and determine if the person's business or ministry philosophy matches yours. Check out the site's statement of faith or values. Also check out the length of time the site has been in business. Evaluating how long the site has been in operation will help you understand the level of risk if you are required to pay a fee.

- Take plenty of time to check out the site without posting or paying so you can make sure that members share your basic values and beliefs and that the feel of the site is positive and matches your preferences.

- Before paying, contact the Better Business Bureau or other consumer sites to see if other online daters have registered complaints.

- Send an e-mail to the site owners or customer care center and ask a question to see if the response you receive reflects godliness and good customer service.

The large secular sites may have millions of members, but you will have to sort through many inquiries from nonbelievers. Those sites tend to ask members only one or two general questions about religion. In contrast, Christian sites tend to ask for more detailed information about a person's faith, such as denomination and level of involvement, as well as open-ended questions regarding the person's relationship with God. But you need to know more than simply whether a site is run by Christians. You need to know whether the other members are compatible with your convictions and beliefs. Women, minorities, and people in smaller denominations are still underrepresented on most online dating sites.

Silently observing the site, sampling profiles of members and messages from the site owner, and even reading chat-room or message-board posts will reveal the site's atmosphere. Observing will also help you get a feel for what is or isn't appropriate to say in each group. Many message boards discourage posts that sound like personal ads. Sometimes members in these groups will not accept instant messages or e-mails from people who don't get involved in the discussions.

They Never Write, They Never Call...

The interpersonal dynamic of online communities is very different from the church down the street. If you expect to join a group and get a flood of e-mails or instant messages saying "Welcome aboard," you'll probably be disappointed. With all their e-mail to wade through, people prioritize what and whom they can respond to. At most churches, if you say hello to people, they will immediately respond and will probably ask your name and seek some information about you. But online, people respond much more judiciously.

With online communication, if you post a profile, send an e-mail, or invite someone to chat in an online community and don't receive a response, it's not quite the same as being ignored. On message boards people may agree with your posts and not tell you so they can avoid sending a boring I-agree post. Or you may post a question or topic for discussion, and it doesn't generate much interest. This is not rejection; it's merely an indication that there is a lot more going on at the site. Timing is everything. You might post the same topic months later and see it generate major discussions.

Bottom line: Chill out. The worst thing you can do is respond in anger to a perceived slight only to find out you were the one who was wrong. Being slow to speak and slow to become angry will keep you from alienating people (see James 1:19).

PRACTICING CYBERSECURITY

Cybersecurity is the most important skill you need in online dating. Many believers wrongly believe that it's unchristian to be suspicious of others, especially if you're dating on a "Christian" Web site. But Jesus tells us that wolves lurk among the sheep, so we need to be shrewd in our dealings with others (see Matthew 10:16).

Other Christians mistakenly believe that taking precautions is the same as living in fear, which the Bible warns against. However, there is a huge difference between living in fear and being shrewd about protecting yourself.

"I believe God will keep me safe, but I also have to do my part," explains Kennedy, a twenty-something woman who met her husband online. "I know this Christian who went away on vacation with a man she met online after only two offline dates. She told me that I was living a life of fear. But I don't think there is anything wrong with being cautious.

"Would you leave your doors unlocked while driving in unfamiliar parts of town? Would you tell everyone all the intimate and personal details about yourself? Well, that's what you are doing when you are online. This time, though, you have invited millions of perfect strangers into your home. Until you meet someone and see him or her walk the talk, you don't know that person. It's not living in fear; it's called behaving wisely."

Kennedy knows about Internet safety because she survived a close call with a predator. He seemed like a normal Christian but turned out to be a man who preys on trusting women. She lost a few hundred dollars and her naiveté, but she learned how to recognize the dangers that exist.

Heed the Safety Rules

When you're online, you need to understand the difference between ungodly fear and God-honoring caution. As you pursue the latter, test the words of those you meet to make sure you see no warning signs that signal deception. (For an in-depth discussion of deception, see chapter 9.) For instance, listen carefully to people's stories about themselves and their lives, and ask them to repeat the stories later in your relationship. Take note of any major discrepancies. If you can't get a straight answer or if something a person tells you seems too good to be true, then he or she may be lying, you may be reading too much into it, or you both may have misunderstood each other.

If you have established a close relationship with someone and he or she doesn't want to send you a picture or meet you, then that person could be posing as someone he or she is not. Also, if someone tries to guilt or shame you for practicing cybersecurity, run! A person who truly cares for you will understand your need to be safe. Finally, if a person tells you that he or she is in love with you and asks you for more personal information than he or she has revealed, then you might be involved with someone who is out to harm or use you. Sure, we all love it when someone takes a deep interest in us and makes us feel special. But cyberspace is full of people who will use information about you for their own selfish and evil benefit. So be careful and put into practice the top three rules for online security:

1. Keep your personal identification information to yourself until you are absolutely sure the other person is legit.
2. Never give out the location or phone number of your home or work until the person is proven to be trustworthy.
3. Never give a person money or other forms of financial assistance. If someone needs financial help, send him or her to a church ministry or social-service organization. Do not mix social service or ministry efforts with online dating.

You should also learn how to recognize unhealthy or abusive people and avoid them. Scripture tells us to test the spirits because many are not from God (see 1 John 4:1). There is nothing wrong with testing those who claim to be believers. Testing means that you evaluate people's online behavior, words, and beliefs to see if they line up with God's Word. If others have said you are too trusting offline, make a mental note to be much more careful online.

"The biggest thing I learned going online was not to allow guilt to force me to talk to guys just because they say they are Christians," says Natalie, a teacher's aide who has been dating online for three years. "I got suspicious of one guy who was trying to make me feel guilty for not wanting to talk. He said, 'I thought Christians are supposed to see the good in others.' I mentioned this guy in an online group and sure enough, he was doing it to other women. One woman said he's looking for someone he can control or intimidate."

If you frequently get hurt or taken advantage of offline, then chances are good that you'll attract unhealthy relationships online. The stakes are higher online because predators know how to hit your emotional hot buttons—such as the desire to be loved, a fear of abandonment, or a need to belong—and get you to let down your defenses. If you don't recognize your emotional hot buttons, you'll be vulnerable to those who want to use you. Without realizing it, you could be doing things that attract people who are wrong for you. A lack of self-awareness will leave you vulnerable.

"I felt like I wasn't being a faithful Christian by being so suspicious of others," says Olivia, a dental hygienist. "Well, until I met Jeff. I kept debating whether to allow him to pick me up at my house for our first date. I'm glad I didn't. In less than a week, he got some revelation from God that I was to be his wife. He became scary and possessive. After a while I had to change my e-mail address because he wouldn't stop harassing me. He turned into a monster when I told him that I didn't want to continue the relationship. I'm glad I protected my home address."

The Lure of Addictions, Porn, and Unhealthy Relationships

Practicing cybersecurity will help you avoid the addictive and ungodly aspects of the Internet. Just as cyberspace can be used to bring together two honest and healthy Christians, it can also weaken you spiritually and lure you into a stronghold of addictive behavior. A growing body of research indicates that using the Internet itself can be addictive. (See chapter 2 to identify any tendencies you may have toward addictive behavior.) Online addiction does not have to involve pornography; it can involve such areas as day trading or simply spending hours every day chatting with others. And, of course, those who are vulnerable to lust and sexual temptation will find easy access to pornography. Many porn sites send unsolicited pictures to those who go to chat rooms or join unmoderated online singles communities and dating sites. (See chapter 9 for a detailed discussion of cybersecurity, including how to recognize your vulnerabilities.

NETSPEAK USED HERE

Netspeak refers to the unique way people use symbols, acronyms, words, and sentence structure to communicate effectively online. For instance, correct spelling and grammar are essential for a good first impression and remain important until you move your relationship offline. Individuals who have problems with spelling and grammar and who are unable to express their emotions clearly in writing will have trouble since no-go decisions are made quickly.

What you say and how you say it are critical to your success online. The person who is reading your words does not have the benefit of seeing your facial expressions, hearing your tone of voice, or interpreting your hand gestures. As a result, it is extremely easy to misunderstand each other. So choose your words carefully and remember that you can't take them back once you hit the Send button. When the other person reads your message, you won't be there to clear up any confusion.

Sometimes the perceived anonymity of the Internet will entice people to behave in ways they would never behave in person. Christians sometimes send rude and unloving e-mails and message-board posts. Religious debates often turn into personal attacks. Far too often the Golden Rule gets trampled in cyberspace.

If you have trouble controlling your anger, don't think you can hide behind the anonymity of cyberspace. Many times a knowledgeable computer user can find out who you are, especially if you have personal identification information in your profile. You must learn to control your anger or frustration even if you believe someone else has been rude or unloving toward you. Never get on a soapbox and try to correct or rebuke strangers online. Just leave the situation alone and move on to the next person. If you don't, you may end up provoking someone to retaliate against you.

When you send messages in cyberspace, you lose all control over how your words are used. When you say something in e-mail, chat, or instant messages, the other person can save your interactions and use them later. So before hitting the Send button, ask yourself whether you would be ashamed or uncomfortable if someone you know saw your message.

"I was in a long-term online relationship with a man who I thought was the strongest Christian I had ever dated," says Carol, a woman who has been dating online for three years. "He was a minister at his church. As we got closer, I began to get uncomfortable with all of his conversations about sex. I know serious couples should talk about sex eventually, but I didn't feel like we had reached that point. When I told him I was uncomfortable, he began to get angry and tell me he wasn't going to marry another woman who had sexual hang-ups. When he hurt my feelings for the last time, I called his church and gave his head minister a copy of the e-mails and chats so the church could see how this man was talking to women online."

Six Deadly Cybersins

In both secular and Christian online communities, several pet peeves are mentioned repeatedly. To improve the effectiveness of your profile, your e-mail, or your instant-message contacts, try to avoid the top six "cybersins" that can kill online communication.

1. *Using all caps, all lowercase, or an odd mixture of caps and lowercase in your message.* Committing this sin guarantees that you'll leave an unfavorable impression. Words typed entirely in caps are hard to read, and people interpret them as shouting. Using all lowercase words leaves the impression that you are too lazy to hit the Shift key. Typing words with an odd mixture of caps and lowercase is just plain bizarre.

2. *Not using acronyms and emoticons properly.* Because you do so much typing with online communication, cyberspace is full of *netcronyms,* acronyms made up of the initial letters from phrases, plus abbreviations of commonly used sentences and phrases, plus phonetic sound-alike words. Sometimes netcronyms are intuitive, but often your best guess could be wrong. Some are unique to a particular Web-site community. If you don't know with certainty what a netcronym stands for, ask someone. The Web-site owner or the Webmaster is a good resource if you feel too embarrassed to ask in a larger group setting. Since there are hundreds of netcronyms, doing a keyword emoticon search should provide you with information about the most commonly used netcronyms and emoticons.

3. *Lashing out in anger.* This happens to people who don't realize they aren't the center of the universe. You might think that once you send an e-mail or post to a message board, you'll receive a quick response. Don't think that. The sin isn't in feeling hurt by not receiving a response. The problem is when you respond in anger. Not being acknowledged is not a judgment against you, so don't take it personally.

4. *Sending e-mails or messages that don't make sense or are too long.* If a person has to spend too much time trying to figure out what you're saying, then you have left a bad impression. So before you hit the Send button, reread your message to make sure you're being clear. Otherwise, you'll just make the person who received your message say, "Huh?" Also, get to the point in your e-mails. Now is not the time to write a novel.

5. *Being overly needy, lonely, or suffocating.* The quickest way to scare

off a potential match is to dwell on how lonely you are or to send excessive amounts of e-mail or instant messages. Equally offensive and scary is to camp out online and then send a flurry of instant messages to the person when he or she logs on. Sometimes people may simply disappear because they don't want to hurt you by rejecting you outright. And sometimes they may disappear because you are scaring them.

6. *Not responding in a timely fashion to e-mails from those you are interested in pursuing.* I know you're busy and probably receive too many e-mails. If you choose to focus on certain ones to the exclusion of others, then accept that you may have missed an opportunity to pursue the people you put on hold. People who receive e-mails from someone they spoke with months ago tend to think the other person is contacting them only because a more promising relationship fell through. If it has been several months since your last contact, just let that person go.

Learn the Rules of Netspeak

On the Internet, the written word is king. And since text-based conversations can't convey body language and other nonverbal signals, people have also created emoticons to convey their feelings. So make sure to learn the rules of Netspeak, including the proper use of emoticons, netcronyms, and other cyberspace-specific jargon. Many terms are exclusive to cyberspace, so if you're new to online communities, take a crash course in this new language.

Following are some common emoticons. You don't have to use any of them, but you'll probably see many of them as you talk to others. You'll also see variations of these and some that are newly developed. (*Note to PC users:* When communicating with Mac users, make sure you turn off the autoformat feature in Word that changes keystrokes to symbols [e.g., Word autoformat will change :-) to ☺.] These symbols don't translate correctly into Mac language and will look like gibberish to your Mac friend.)

:-)	smile
:-(	sad
;-)	winking, just kidding
:-P	sticking out your tongue
:-D	big smile, laughing
:-O	surprise
:-@	screaming
:(	frowning
>:->	angry
:-*	kiss
:-**	returning a kiss
()	hugs
((()))	big hugs
:'-C	crying
:->	sarcastic
:-v	the person is talking
:-(0)	the person is yelling
:-}	nervous smile
:o[	not impressed
:-)}	trying not to laugh
:-c	depressed
:( ) =	can't stop talking
:-))	very happy
:o}	bashful or embarrassed
:-/	grim
:-&	tongue-tied
O0o:-)	thinking

Here are a few basic netcronyms:

a/s/l?	age/sex/location?
AFK	away from the keyboard
BAK	back at the keyboard
BCNU	be seeing you
BF	boyfriend
BRB	be right back
BTW	by the way
F2F	face to face
FWIW	for what it's worth
FYA	for your amusement
GMTA	great minds think alike
HB	hurry back
HHOK	ha ha, only kidding
HTH	hope this helps
IMHO	in my humble opinion
IMO	in my opinion
JMHO	just my humble opinion
LOL	laughing out loud
NP	no problem
OIC	oh, I see
OTOH	on the other hand
ROTFL	rolling on the floor laughing
TTYL	talk to you later

What (Not) to Talk About

As you learn the language of cyberspace, get to know which issues and topics are inappropriate for online discussion. Most sensitive topics—past abuse, family problems, and an explanation of disabilities or chronic illnesses—should be discussed in a setting that allows the other person to at least hear your voice. Even better, choose a setting that allows the other person to see your facial expressions. (For an in-depth discussion of dealing with sensitive subjects, see chapter 10.)

To add a visual dimension to online communication, some people use a Web cam and discuss sensitive issues via a video chat. However, computers can get hung up when Web cams are being used, and sometimes unnatural delays can occur in the flow of the conversation. You might get frustrated when you launch a deep discussion and then end up spending your time trying to maintain your connection. Bottom line: Some topics are just too hard to explain without using the telephone or talking in person.

When you are equipped with the rules of the cyber-road, including cyberstyle, cybersecurity, and Netspeak, you are prepared to communicate clearly and safely on the Internet. Not only will these skills enable you to make a much better impression on others, but they will vastly increase your chances of finding your best match online.

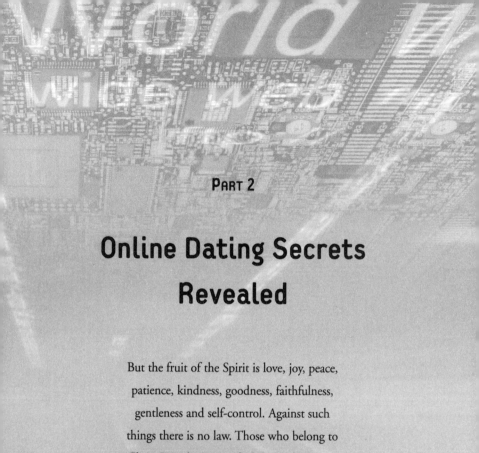

PART 2

Online Dating Secrets Revealed

But the fruit of the Spirit is love, joy, peace,
patience, kindness, goodness, faithfulness,
gentleness and self-control. Against such
things there is no law. Those who belong to
Christ Jesus have crucified the sinful nature
with its passions and desires. Since we live
by the Spirit, let us keep in step with the
Spirit. Let us not become conceited,
provoking and envying each other.

—Galatians 5:22-26

Five

Looking for Love in All the Right Places

Knowing Where to Look and Whom You're Looking For

I remember going fishing as a child. I thought I could just plop anything into the water and come home with catfish to eat. Wrong. You plop just anything in the wrong place, and you'll end up having to eat catfish at a restaurant on the way home. Fishing enthusiasts bring home more fish because they do their homework and make the right preparations. They learn the habits, the movements, and the habitats of the fish they want to catch. Armed with that knowledge, they cast their lines in those spots, and they are successful.

The same general principle applies to online dating. You're wasting your time if you're not introducing yourself at sites that have members who most closely approximate your desired match. If you aren't receiving responses from enough people who are compatible with you, you could be fishing in the wrong lake.

A fisherman knows how to attract the best fish once he or she finds the right lake. Likewise, you need to create the best first impression with the people you talk to online. Read on to find out how to cast your net to catch better fish.

WHERE TO FIND A MATCH

To find like-minded singles in cyberspace, you have to know where to look. Web sites tend to come and go, so I won't try to provide you with a list of specific sites. But most of the active dating sites can be found by plugging keywords into a search engine, such as *google.com*. As previously mentioned, keywords like "Christian singles" or "Christian dating" should bring up the most popular and largest online dating sites. If you're looking for dating sites with specific demographics, such as those within your church denomination, then add keywords to your search: Christian singles + Presbyterian, for instance. You will likely receive many results, so you may want to enclose your keywords in quotation marks to get exact matches rather than variations of each word (e.g., "Singles" + "Presbyterian").

If you want to find Christian singles' chat rooms or message boards, you'll have to be more targeted in your search. Check your Internet Service Provider (ISP) to see if there are existing chat rooms or message boards that suit your needs. Some of the most popular places for Christian singles' message boards and chat rooms are found on *yahoo.com*. But great groups also exist on *msn.com* and *aol.com*. Many online dating sites also provide chat rooms and message boards for their members.

As mentioned in chapter 4, you can also meet other singles in cyberspace through matchmaker sites, online ad sites, chat rooms, message boards, and Internet game sites. Let's look more closely at each of these options.

Matchmaker Sites

Most people use the terms *online dating* and *matchmaker sites* interchangeably. For our purposes, however, we will define a *matchmaker site* as an impartial third party that possesses extensive profile capabilities and uses information gathered about your personality, religious beliefs, and other individual preferences to match you behind the scenes with other singles who are most compatible with you. True matchmaker sites don't allow members to search profiles of other members on their own. You must wait for the matchmaker to introduce you to other members who most closely match your preferences.

Matchmaking sites can be compared to cultures in which parents turn to a third party to find suitable spouses for their children. Although it's not an exact comparison, the basic underlying principle of using a third party to facilitate a match is the same. As in cultures where matches are arranged, many online daters prefer matchmaker sites because they don't want to wade through thousands of profiles just to find the few people who are compatible with them.

The largest and most popular matchmaker site is *eharmony.com.*

Online Ad Sites

Large numbers of people use online ad sites to find prospective matches. In fact, this is the most common way people search for others. On these sites, daters can post their preferences, screen profiles of other members, initiate contact with those they're interested in, and respond to open-ended questions without having to go through a third party. These sites range from large, general networks to sites that are specific to particular church denominations and other unique niche markets. Many people prefer these sites since the large number of members enables them to choose from a broader field. This advantage can also be a disadvantage, however, since searching for a match can be very time consuming. Some of the larger sites are: *match.com, personals.yahoo.com* (secular sites), and *adammeeteve.com, christiancafe.com, bigchurch.com,* and *christian.soulmate.com* (Christian sites). You'll have to do your homework to see if these sites meet your needs.

Chat Rooms

These real-time interactive forums enable singles to chat online with other like-minded singles. Forums are sometimes organized by topic, and as many as fifty people can participate in real-time conversations. Conversations are often fast-paced and are sometimes disjointed because so many people are talking at once. Participants can see everyone else's typed comments, and not everyone is talking about the same thing. Sadly, chats in Christian singles communities tend to be targets for pornographic spammers. This is also true of some chat rooms hosted by AOL, Yahoo! and other ISPs. Typically, the safer chat rooms are found in online communities with restricted memberships where the chat rooms have hands-on moderators to control the pornographers and hatemongers.

In general, chat room members resist using this forum for dating purposes because the conversations are open to everyone, but people can sometimes become attracted to another member based on the way that person expresses him- or herself online. Individuals who sense chemistry during a chat room conversation can move a conversation to a private chat room or use instant messages so they can talk with each other without disruptions from the chat of others.

Message Boards

These are online forums or groups organized by topic and/or demographic group. Members post messages regarding a topic of discussion, and that message remains on the board for a period of time so that interested members can read and respond to it. Members don't have to be present at a certain time to share in the discussion.

These forums allow for lively debate, the sharing of information, requests for advice and support, and opportunities to make friends with people from all over the world. Message boards also are known as discussion boards, listservs, electronic bulletin boards, and threaded conversations. As with chat rooms, message boards are not intended for dating purposes; however, Christian singles sometimes meet matches when they notice posts that reveal a like-minded person. They can then move their conversation to more private forums such as private chat, e-mail, and instant messaging.

Popular message boards for Christian singles can be found on *yahoo* *.com, msn.com,* and *aol.com.*

Internet Game Sites

Some people meet while playing chess, dominoes, bingo, or other games on Internet game sites. Many game sites have chat rooms associated with them so you can chat with others while playing, even if it's a one-person game. Typically these sites are not geared specifically toward Christian singles, so if you do meet a fellow believer in this manner, it's a rare occurrence. The largest game sites are at *pogo.com* and *yahoo.com.*

CHOOSING THE BEST SITE

Most singles have a definite preference regarding which type of Web site or forum they want to join. It helps to list your criteria and evaluate your preferences in advance. Here are some of the key areas of preference:

Cost or membership fee. If a fee-based site will not allow you a trial period for searching and viewing profiles, then move on. You should be able to get a feel for the type of members at the site before deciding whether it's worth the fee. However, most sites that allow free searching on a trial basis require you to become a paid member before you can send an e-mail to a member of the dating site.

Level of personal control. This refers to whether you are free to conduct your own search or whether the site conducts the search by matching your profile with other compatible profiles. Some matchmaker sites send matches to you that they have determined are compatible with your profile and personality. However, many people still prefer making their own case-by-case choices. You need to decide how much control you want to retain.

Interactivity. Some sites limit your activity to searching profiles and sending e-mail. Others require that you do nothing while you wait for the matchmaker service to come up with a match. If you want to join in message-board or chat-room discussions, look for sites that provide options for interacting with other members. Some interactive opportunities allow members to spend time in a virtual singles group to make friends while the search process is going on.

Anonymity and security. The most important consideration is the ability to protect your identity until *you* are ready to reveal it. Most dating sites allow you to send double-blind e-mails so that only the Web site's system knows your actual e-mail address. The person receiving your e-mail sees only your member ID. Some sites require you to access the Web site itself to send and receive e-mails. Other sites forward e-mail to your actual e-mail address. If the site you choose does the latter, then be careful not to hit the Reply button from your personal e-mail account. Instead, go back to the Web site and send your reply within its secured system. Some sites allow members to interact using anonymous chat and instant-messaging capabilities.

Centrality of faith and religious affiliation. If you prefer to use secular sites, it will probably take longer to find suitable Christians who meet your criteria for an ideal match. Some singles only want to be involved with sites that are owned and run by Christians. Since Christian-operated Web sites come and go, be careful about becoming a paid member until you get a sense of how stable the site is. Also, check the site's statement of faith to make sure it reflects your own beliefs. Some sites are run by members of certain church denominations and will attract more members with that affiliation. If you suspect that a self-described "Christian" Web site is owned by a secular company, check for a statement of faith or a mission statement.

Moderated or unmoderated. You won't fully appreciate the involvement of sensitive and prayerful moderators until you slip into a site that is not moderated. Unmoderated sites have no standards at all, so members can attach any picture to their profiles, say anything in their profiles, and send e-mails or instant messages that contain any content. They can also post any message and say absolutely anything in a chat room.

Moderated sites tend to maintain high standards and take seriously the protection of their members. Moderators typically review every membership applicant to ensure that the prospective member is not a known Net troublemaker or a pornographer. Moderators review and approve profiles, pictures, and any subsequent changes to make sure they are appropriate. Some Web site moderators monitor message boards and approve messages before they are posted or distributed to the group. Others remove objectionable posts. Moderated Web sites also tend to monitor online behavior and give members a way to report those who may be harassing them.

Group size and composition. Some people prefer the coziness of a small group; others seek a group that is characterized by racial diversity; varying ages, religious affiliations, or educational backgrounds, or a wide range of hobbies or interests. If group size and composition are important to you, then spend time hanging out at Web sites and interact with some of the members to get a feel for whether you really belong in the group.

Indicate your own preferences in the following chart:

Online Search Preferences			
Areas of Preference	*Extremely Important*	*Moderately Important*	*Not Important*
Cost or Membership Fee			
Level of Personal Control			
Interactivity			
Anonymity and Security			
Centrality of Faith and Religious Affiliation			
Moderated or Unmoderated			
Group Size and Composition			

How the Sites Measure Up

Now that you know your online search preferences, you have the information you need to select the sites that will be the best places for you to meet someone. The summaries to follow will help you weigh the pros and cons so you can determine which type of site will meet your needs.

Matchmaker Sites

Cost. Matchmaker sites usually charge for their services. These sites can be the most expensive among the online dating options.

Control. On matchmaker sites, members have little control over the matches they are sent. However, members can affect matches based on the responses they give to the site's screening quizzes or by changing their profiles or preferences. Individual members typically can't search the profiles of other members but have to rely instead upon the matchmaker service to send them compatible matches. Nevertheless, many singles find great benefit in having a third party send them prescreened, compatible matches to consider.

Interactivity. The level of interactivity on matchmaker sites tends to be low and is confined to the matches that are sent to you for consideration. Once a match is sent and both members want to make contact, the interaction follows a structured, controlled format in the beginning. This structure helps members pace themselves during the early stages of a relationship. When the relationship reaches a certain stage, members are able to have free-flowing conversations.

Anonymity and security. Matchmaker sites tend to be extremely secure and provide members with the proper level of anonymity.

Centrality of faith and religious affiliation. As of this writing, the true matchmaker sites are not exclusively Christian, although many operate according to faith-based principles. Membership tends to be open to both believers and nonbelievers.

Moderated or unmoderated. These types of sites tend to be carefully controlled and monitored.

Group size and composition. The cost of this type of service might skew the membership toward a higher-income demographic; thus, it may not be representative of the larger society. You might find a disproportionate number of professionals and possibly fewer young adults on these sites, for instance.

Online Ad Sites

Cost. The fees for these sites vary widely. They typically allow for free searches and posting of profiles, but a paid membership is required before you can conduct advanced searches or communicate with members. Most of these sites allow you to search profiles during a trial period before paying a membership fee.

Control. Members are in charge of their own matches from the universe of member profiles. However, searching through all the profiles can be time consuming and frustrating, particularly if you end up finding only a few suitable matches.

Interactivity. Many online ad sites have interactive elements, such as internal message boards and chat rooms.

Anonymity and security. Most ad sites offer secured and anonymous e-mails.

Centrality of faith and religious affiliation. As more Christians enter the online dating market, there will likely be an increase in the number of sites for specific church denominations. Christian sites allow for a more detailed description of faith-based preferences that are given only cursory attention on secular sites.

Moderated or unmoderated. Online ad sites vary in how strictly they monitor profiles, pictures, chats, and e-mails. Some sites prevent members from making even small modifications to their profiles without approval. Others don't screen any changes.

Group size and composition. The composition and size of these sites vary according to the specificity of their target demographic group and how many of the members in this target group are engaged in online dating.

Chat Rooms, Message Boards, and Internet Game Sites

Chat rooms, message boards, and game sites are not typically the most efficient way to meet eligible Christian singles. These forums are better suited to general social interaction and friendship building. It's possible, however, to develop chemistry with another person in these forums. Typically, chemistry develops over time as one person observes another person's posts about their thoughts, attitudes, beliefs, and views.

Cost. These types of sites are generally free, but they sometimes include advertising. On some of the game sites, paid members can escape the advertising.

Control. Most people who use these sites have minimal profiles that lack detailed and specific personal information. Unless the chat rooms or message boards are specifically designated for Christian singles, you will interact with nonbelievers and married adults as well.

Interactivity. These types of sites offer the highest level of interactivity and communication with other members. In chat rooms, many Christians find support and friendship without the pressure of being on a dating site.

Anonymity and security. Unless you choose to hide your e-mail address and name, others can easily contact you through instant messaging and e-mails. With some ISPs like AOL, all someone needs to know is your screen name (the nickname you choose for online activities) in order to locate you without your permission or knowledge whenever you are in an AOL-sponsored chat room or on a message board.

Centrality of faith and religious affiliation. Game sites are typically secular; however, chat rooms and message boards range from secular to religious to specifically Christian.

Moderated or unmoderated. These types of sites can either be moderated or unmoderated. Christian singles are wise to avoid unmoderated chat rooms or message boards to escape becoming a target for spammers and pornographers.

Group size and composition. Chat rooms, message boards, and game sites tend to be large and diverse. For general Christian singles groups, however, too much diversity can cause problems due to disagreements that arise when Christians passionately defend their doctrines or religious affiliations.

Your Ideal Match

To improve your chances of finding a great match, you'll need to be specific in listing the qualities you are looking for. Christian? Yes. Breathing? Yes. Someone who shares your faith and interests? Of course. That's a good start, but it's not even close to serving the purpose of helping you find your ideal match.

Online dating allows you the perfect opportunity to dig deeper and identify exactly what you consider to be the critical qualities in a spouse. You can run a search based on those qualities, but first you have to know which qualities are most important to you. Another reason to articulate what you are looking for is that it helps you develop a systematic and organized way to screen and evaluate the people you meet. Digging deeper will also help you clarify your must-have qualities in a spouse and distinguish them from qualities you consider optional or might even waive on a case-by-case basis.

To successfully navigate the online-dating process, you will need a plan for screening and evaluating the people you interact with. The best approach is to develop an objective measure that is based on qualities you consider essential and others that you can take or leave, depending on the person you meet.

The Essential Qualities Matrix on pages 84-87 will help you systematically evaluate your matches and refine your preferences. First, determine your own attitudes and preferences. Then describe the essential qualities of your ideal match. Note which qualities are nonnegotiable and which are optional. For the nonnegotiable qualities, make sure you can explain to yourself why this quality is so important to you. If you have trouble coming up with a reason, then reexamine whether this is truly an essential quality. The more nonnegotiable qualities you list, the fewer suitable matches you will find.

The Physical Dimension

The physical realm involves much more than a person's height, weight, and age. Also worth considering are a person's clothing preference, how much makeup, perfume, or jewelry a woman wears, and the presence of body art and piercings. If you are a classy dresser in a high-profile occupation, you may not want someone who hates to dress up. Men and women may also have differing attitudes about the amount of makeup women may use.

Another area to consider is the level of a person's physical activity. If you are an outdoor enthusiast, then you'll want to know if a potential match prefers to stay indoors watching television or reading a book. If regular fitness activities are a requirement for you, then be up-front about that. An underexplored area in this category is a person's diet and his or her attitudes toward food. For instance, if someone is a strict vegetarian, he or she may have trouble in a relationship with a meat-and-potatoes person.

You also need to determine if a person currently smokes, drinks, or takes drugs, or if he or she has a history of these behaviors. Can you live with a smoker or with someone who drinks alcohol? If so, how much of this behavior—such as an occasional social drink or a glass of wine every evening—are you comfortable with? What if you discovered your match used illicit drugs in the past? How long would the person need to have been free of substance abuse before you would consider him or her as a viable marriage partner?

The Essential Qualities Matrix		
	Quality	*I Am…*
Physical	Age	
	Race	
	Appearance: body type, fitness, clothing preference, use of makeup, body art	
	Level of physical activity	
	Diet and attitudes about food	
	Smoking, alcohol, drugs— current and past usage	
	Emotional health	
	Physical health	
	Sexual history: virgin? past sexual abuse, etc.	
Economic, Educational, Political	Occupation and employment status	
	Salary	
	Financial health: debt, bankruptcy, child support, etc.	
	Location and distance willing to travel for a match	
	Attitudes toward money: saving, spending, etc.	
	Living situation: own, rent, live with family	
	Level of education	
	Political views/affiliations	
	Level of political involvement	

The Essential Qualities Matrix	
My Ideal Match Is...	*Essential or Optional Trait?*

(continued)

The Essential Qualities Matrix		
	Quality	*I Am...*
Social and Personal	Martial history: never married, divorced, widowed	
	Number of children (including number still living at home)	
	Desire to have children and number desired	
	Pets and attitude about pets	
	Personality type	
	Child-rearing attitudes, family history, upbringing	
	Attitudes toward displays of affection	
	Temperament and how negative emotions are expressed	
	Top interests/hobbies	
Religious	Religious affiliation	
	Length of time as a Christian	
	Church attendance (frequency)	
	Core religious beliefs and practices	
	Spiritual gifts	
	Ministry interest (current and desired)	
	Worship-style preference	
	Views on women's roles in the home and at church	

The Essential Qualities Matrix	
My Ideal Match Is...	*Essential or Optional Trait?*

Finally, you need to consider the area of health. Are there some emotional or physical illnesses or disorders that you could not deal with? Would your interest wane if you discovered the person had a history of depression, an eating disorder, or cancer? What about sexual history? Have you ever been sexually abused? What are your preferences for the type of sex within marriage? Do you require your match to be a virgin? The sexual questions are tricky because they are not appropriate to discuss in the beginning stages of a relationship. But they are extremely important to discuss if the two of you are seriously considering marriage. To maintain purity and accountability, however, these types of discussions are best handled in premarital counseling with a Christian counselor or minister.

The Economic, Educational, and Political Dimensions

People who have strong preferences regarding the occupation of a potential match are not necessarily concerned about status, money, or power. Many people don't want to become involved with someone who is a first responder—police officer, firefighter, or paramedic—because of the stresses and dangers associated with these jobs. Some do not wish to be spouses of military personnel, ministers, or missionaries because of frequent moves. Many people find it difficult to date someone who is unemployed. Also, salary issues are tricky and should not be discussed too early in a relationship for security reasons. But it's important to discuss views on whether it's appropriate for a woman to make more money than her husband does, for instance.

Money also becomes an issue when a couple's attitudes toward saving, spending, and debt are incompatible. Another concern is financial health. If you have good credit, how do you feel about being involved with someone who is in deep debt, has had a bankruptcy, or is paying child support? Finances also factor into decisions about long-distance relationships. Frequent travel, lodging, meals on the road, and other travel-related expenses might make a long-distance relationship untenable.

For many people, education or even intellect is important. However, this dimension does not necessarily need to be restricted to degrees or types of schools attended. Many people are simply looking for a match who loves to learn. This can be reflected in the types of books a person reads or the continuing education courses, seminars, or workshops a person attends. Do you prefer matches who have completed a certain level of formal education, or are you looking for matches who just love to learn? What role does intelligence or wit play in your preferences for an ideal match?

Finally, you must consider your political views and the strength of your political convictions. Can you be happy with someone who holds opposing views and is active in political causes, such as campaigns or protests?

The Social and Personal Dimensions

How important to you is a person's marital history and status and the number of children he or she has, including the number of children still living at home? Although people may change their minds about the desire for and number of additional children, you might still want to get a good feel for how adamant the person is about those preferences. Never enter a relationship with the expectation that you will change the other person's views or preferences.

Also, explore your own attitudes about child rearing. You want to know how the other person was raised and what he or she considers the best child-rearing philosophy. If you are at opposite extremes on this issue, that will definitely cause problems.

Aside from children, there is the question of pets. Pet owners tend to have intense emotional attachments to animals, but not *every* animal. Cat lovers may not mesh with dog lovers. And if a potential match is allergic to pets, is that a deal breaker?

Finally, consider whether your personalities are compatible. If you are a people person, do you prefer another person similar to you or someone who is quieter and more laid-back? What type of sense of humor do you prefer, and what drives you up a wall? What about the person's temperament? Is he or she cheerful and bubbly, quiet and solitary, optimistic or just the opposite? Equally important is how the other person expresses negative emotions. If you express negative emotions by pulling away while the other person becomes more talkative and demanding, there could be a big problem.

The Spiritual Dimension

Secular dating Web sites ask for a person's religious affiliation and may include a general question about church attendance. Sometimes the religious affiliation options are limited to large categories such as Jewish, Christian, Muslim, or Buddhist.

Christian sites tend to ask more in-depth questions, and the religious affiliation section is detailed. They also ask when and how you became a Christian, your frequency of church attendance, and the extent of your ministry involvement. The denomination-specific sites request even more detailed information, such as worship-style preference or attitudes about women's roles in the church and home.

You need to go beyond denominational affiliation, however, and determine which core religious beliefs and practices are central to your faith. If you believe Christians should take Communion every Sunday, use wine for Communion, and drink out of the same chalice, then keep that in mind when you begin communicating with others by e-mail or in chat rooms. Gather information on these core beliefs so that you can make a better go-or-no-go decision.

A final faith-related area to consider is a person's current and desired ministry involvement and interests. If you meet someone who longs to be a foreign missionary, take that desire seriously. Don't think that his or her dream will simply go away. Can you see yourself as the spouse of a missionary? Likewise, could you marry someone who does not have compatible spiritual gifts or who does not desire to participate in the ministry you are most passionate about?

THE MATTER OF GOD-CHOSEN MATES

Christians believe that God is involved in the process of finding their mate. But has God really ordained or chosen just one particular person to be your mate? The notion of God's choosing just one person as your perfect match probably comes from the Creation account in Genesis when God created Eve and gave her to Adam. Or perhaps the idea comes from Genesis 24 when Abraham's servant journeyed to another country to select a bride for Isaac. Overwhelmed by the task, the servant asked God to select the right woman, and God singled out Rebekah.

Many Christians go online with the belief that God has chosen one particular person to be their spouse, and when they meet that person, they'll "know." People who hold this view can become confused when either of two possibilities occurs: (1) they meet more than one person who matches their vision of a God-chosen mate, or (2) their match does not agree with them that God has chosen them for each other. One person may be certain that God desires for them to marry, while the other person is still questioning and may even walk away from the relationship.

I would never say that God does not choose mates for people. But

Scripture teaches that we have a free will, and with that freedom we make choices in many areas of life, including whom we marry. Even if you are certain that God smiles upon your relationship, if the other person exercises free will and walks away from you, there is not much you can do about it. Using Scripture to try to convince the person that he or she is wrong will not work.

Christian singles who believe they have found their one, God-chosen mate need to search their hearts to determine if this revelation is indeed from God or if it is fueled by an overwhelming desire to marry. In an Internet environment, people tend to develop intimate relationships quickly. If you are not experienced in online dating, you might wrongly assume that an intense, surprising emotional attachment to someone is a sign that God has chosen this person as your spouse. Further, if you believe that God has created just one perfect person for you, then you will experience tremendous heartache if an amazing connection turns out to be a misfire. In contrast, those who believe that God can bless any one of many relationships between Christians will tend to pick themselves up from an online rejection and move on with continued hope.

Avoid telling another person that you believe he or she is your chosen mate unless you are sure that both of you feel the same way. If you honestly believe that God has brought the two of you together, relax and take your time. Allow the relationship to grow at its own pace as God guides and directs both of you in seeking His will.

The Soul-Mate Question

If you pursue online dating, you will quickly run into talk about soul mates—finding a soul mate, seeking a soul mate, wondering where a person's soul mate can be found. It goes on and on.

More often than not, Christians use this term to describe a kindred spirit—someone with whom you develop a close soul connection. While the term tends to be used in romantic relationships, others have used it to describe any relationship that reaches to the level of the soul. Such a meaning is consistent with the deep friendship between David and Jonathan in the Old Testament (see 1 Samuel 18:1-3).

However, the popular idea of a soul mate closely parallels a new-age notion that individual souls are incomplete and, as a result, make a separate search for another soul that will complete them. According to this view, a full life does not occur until two souls come together. Hollywood popularizes this notion. Remember when Tom Cruise tells Renée Zellweger in *Jerry Maguire* that she "completes" him? Many Christians fall for this, failing to realize that they *already* have a full and complete life in Christ. Missing that truth, they wait for an ideal spouse to come along so they can move their lives out of a holding pattern.

Claim the riches Christ has given you, including the truth that you are already complete in Him. And don't jump to conclusions about finding your soul mate. Pray during each step of the process and ask God to guide you. Be open to His leading, but don't make assumptions about His choice of this or that person as your mate. Soul mate or not, both of you have to feel God's leading. God has given each of us a free will to make decisions based on living in obedience to Him.

Six

Your Identity in Cyberspace

Revealing Your Heart in a Personal Profile

You can change many things about yourself—such as growing in godly character—but your basic personality and temperament, your strengths and natural abilities remain largely unchanged over a lifetime. You are who God made you.

And that's a good thing. The psalmist said we are "fearfully and wonderfully made" (Psalm 139:14) according to God's design and His desires for each of us. So rejoice in who you are and what you are.

Often it's difficult to relax and be ourselves when others are getting to know us, whether we're in a business setting, at a party with friends, at church, or in the neighborhood. Sometimes we feel exposed when we are called upon to show others who we are. *If I reveal my true self, will I be rejected? If I share what's on my heart, will others denigrate my feelings?*

These are tough questions, and it's good that we don't take them lightly. It's never easy to just relax and be yourself, especially around new people who don't already know your good qualities and value you as a person. So as you begin dating online, a natural concern will be how you present yourself to others.

Your first impression, in many instances, will be made through your profile. But how can you fill out a profile if you hate talking about yourself?

Or perhaps you've already created a profile, but you're now unhappy with it. How can you revise it to capture who you really are? If you have tried online dating and have found that many of the people who contact you are nowhere close to your ideal match, perhaps it's time to take a closer look at how you are presenting yourself.

This Is You in Cyberspace

The version of you that others see in cyberspace has three components. First, your screen name says much about who you are: playful, straightforward, or no-nonsense. Next, of course, is your personal profile. This one is tougher than choosing a screen name since it's detailed and might include a photo. And third is the way you describe your ideal match. This one is tricky because you're setting parameters that will include some people and exclude many others. The choices you make in these three areas form a first impression in the minds of those who "meet" you in cyberspace. And these choices will largely determine whom you are able to meet for online dates.

The cyberspace version of you communicates many things that you don't even realize, such as your level of self-esteem and emotional health, the strength of your faith, and how confident you are. Since you control how you will present yourself, think about how you're coming across to others and take the time necessary to develop a compelling and honest cyberspace introduction. The more careful and thoughtful you are in presenting yourself, the more attractive you will be to others. If you start receiving responses from people who don't come close to fitting your ideal match, go back and tweak your profile to reflect more accurately what you are looking for in a match and how you want to present yourself. Tweaking your profile does not mean fabricating appealing details about yourself. You should aim for being honest and as clear as possible about your ideal match. The less clear you are, the more responses you will receive from those who are nowhere near your ideal match.

Remember, success in online dating requires you to be creative, positive, interesting, and honest. Avoid using an inappropriate or boring screen name, don't create a sloppy profile, and by all means, never under any circumstances post an unflattering picture. Attract the best matches by letting others know that you are worth finding.

WHAT'S IN A SCREEN NAME?

Your choice of a screen name tells others much about your emotional and spiritual health, your faith commitment, and your cyberstyle. People whose screen names reflect creativity, personality, and style are viewed more favorably. Make sure the impressions others are forming about you match your intentions and your character.

A screen name such as "Mr_gentleman" or "Poli_Sci_Grrl" won't be viewed as warm and fuzzy. "Cuteandadorable" and "chivalry_personified" sound conceited, even if they are true. And while "hischildforever" sends the positive message that faith is important to you, using a screen name such as "bornagainchick" sounds a bit over the top. To lighten things up and show your creativity, it's good to engage your sense of humor. Whatever you choose, make sure your screen name does not undermine your Christian witness.

Many singles incorporate religious meaning in their screen names. But if you go that route, avoid the overused terms such as "Proverbs31," "godsman," or "John316." Also, avoid gender-specific terms such as anything with "girl," "mom," "babe," or "chick" in it. Terms like these, especially the last two, are invitations for pornographers or ungodly men to contact you. For men, the most overused terms include "warrior" and anything with "man" in it.

As you settle on a screen name, make sure you're not shouting, "I'm lonely; I'm desperate; PLEASE pay attention to me!" I mean, how many variations on "lonely" are there? We already have enough "lonelyincali" or "nicelonelygirl" or "greatbutlonely" folks out there. Most people are not attracted to those who define themselves by their distraught emotional state.

Finally, make sure your screen name is accurate without divulging too much information. Don't incorporate your birth date, address, or phone number. Also, don't use your entire name, your first name, or any combination of your name and location, such as a house number or ZIP code. Using "David_Jones" or "CathyinOakland" defeats the purpose of cyber-security since you're revealing too much to spammers.

Use a name that keeps your identity and location hidden until you get to know someone well enough to give your real name. This is not paranoia. When you give your name, a person can do a search of your e-mail headers, narrow your location, and run a search of your name and location. Often, your address and telephone number—and even a map to your home—will pop up with just a few clicks of the mouse.

SHOW SOME STYLE

Style issues are a little more technical, but they are still important. Men tend to use their first name followed by a string of numbers. Guys, I'll give it to you straight: "Charles7777777" and "Jack2003" are boring. Also, when you choose a screen name, check how the name flows. Even if you're a big fan of the first lunar landing in 1969 or your birth date is June 9, avoid using the numerals "69" in your screen name. The same rationale applies for avoiding "chick," "hot," or "babe." Such words and numbers invite porn spammers. Also, some combinations of abbreviations spell out a slang word, a racist term, or other objectionable words.

Before you finalize your cybername, ask yourself,

- Does this screen name set me apart from the millions of others who are dating online?
- Does it reveal something about my heart, my faith, and my interests?
- Is this name creative and memorable?

THE PHOTO: TO POST OR NOT TO POST

Adding a picture to your personal profile is a sensitive issue. Some people object to posting photos because they believe that Christians should not place unnecessary emphasis on outward appearance. Others object to photos because they can be deceptive. Many online daters post photos taken years earlier or use so-called glamour shots that have been retouched or taken with special lighting.

Those who argue in favor of posting a picture note that people tend to want a visual representation of who the other person is. It does make corresponding by e-mail more personal. We all form a mental picture of those we can't see, such as a customer or business associate we know only from talking on the telephone. We do the same thing when e-mailing someone we've never met. If I picture you as a tall, athletic person with a full head of hair, and you're actually short, pudgy, and balding, it will be a shock when we meet in person.

Men stress that it's hard for them to connect emotionally with someone unless they have some visual clues. No matter how much we talk about appreciating a person's heart and soul, few relationships develop beyond simple friendship unless there is *some* degree of physical attraction (and only you can define what is attractive). You don't have to be Ben Affleck or Beyoncé to be attractive to others.

Others feel that a photo helps guard against being deceived by the other person. Many online daters have been burned when people describe themselves less than accurately in their profiles. Men complain that women misrepresent their weight and build, while women complain that men gloss over their age and height. That's why many online daters insist on at least two recent pictures at the beginning to verify that the person they are bonding with is being honest.

Regardless of your preference, statistics show that profiles posted with a photo receive 75 percent more "hits" than those without pictures. Plus, people who post pictures receive more e-mail contacts. If you decide not to post a photo, realize that it may take longer for you to get responses. You will also be frequently asked to send a picture before others will agree to talk to you. By choosing not to post, however, you will sift out those who don't share your views on getting to know people independent of their physical appearance. But decide in advance that you won't get bent out of shape by those who refuse to correspond with you unless you send a photo.

Your Cyberface

If you decide to post a picture of yourself, remember that the wrong photo can shut you down right in your tracks. Thomas, a banker in Houston, posted his profile and photo on several Christian dating sites and also joined the Christian message board that I moderate. After sending out almost a hundred e-mails trying to introduce himself, he grew more and more discouraged by the lack of response. Thomas is not unattractive. He is also a personable and witty Christian who is mature in his faith. And his posts on the message board were always a hit among other members.

So why weren't people responding? I checked out his profile on all the sites where he was a member. He posted the same picture on all the sites, and since I had seen him in person, I gasped at his choice for his cyberface. His photo made him look like a felon on death row. Thomas was scaring women away by choosing the wrong picture. After he posted a more flattering picture, he began meeting with success.

Use the following Profile Photo Checklist to help you choose your best primary and secondary photos.

Profile Photo Checklist

____ Choose a recent photo that accurately reflects who you are today. If you've gained or lost weight or experienced other physical changes, such as graying or loss of hair, post a picture that reflects your most flattering current look.

____ Make sure the primary picture provides a clear, focused view of your face. Your secondary picture can be a full-length or more candid shot.

____ Keep the picture focused on you—don't include your children, friends, or anyone else. Also refrain from pictures where you crop out your ex, unless you make sure there isn't some phantom hand on your shoulder or a stray ear showing on the edge of the photo.

____ Dress modestly. No bathing suits, bare chests, tank tops, halters, midriff shirts, lowrider jeans, baggy jeans with boxer shorts exposed, low-cut tops, tight-fitting clothing, or short skirts. Pornographic spammers survey singles profiles, and you may become a target if you don't choose your clothing wisely.

____ Don't dress for yard work or auto repair. Men, don't post or send a picture of yourself in a sweaty T-shirt, a greasy sweatshirt, a sloppy flannel shirt, or even worse, your undershirt. Show some respect for the other person.

___ Go for candid shots over stiff studio portraits. People prefer to get to know the everyday you, not the you who's dressed for a formal dinner party.

___ No Web-cam or driver's-license pictures! Borrow a camera or buy a disposable camera to take good pictures of yourself. You can have your picture placed on a CD-ROM, or you can scan them. Most online dating sites will scan at least one picture for you at no charge.

___ Monitor what is visible in your photo. Do you have clutter all around, a stack of dirty dishes, a car on concrete blocks?

___ Smile. Ask yourself if your picture shows joy in your life.

POSTING A PROFILE: ARE YOU WORTH FINDING?

Don't take your profile description too lightly. You've known yourself all your life, so you may feel that you don't need a lot of description. But the millions of strangers in cyberspace have no idea who you are. So make sure you write a thorough profile—but don't write a book.

Get it clear in your mind what you're trying to accomplish. Imagine yourself at a singles get-together. What would you wear and what would you say to someone you find interesting? Would you talk about your ex and your recent breakup, how much you have to pay in child support, or how your boss is unsympathetic about the mess you're going through? No. Would you talk about how much you hate your current circumstances and what you'd give just to have a normal married life like everyone else? No. Would you talk about how angry and depressed you are and why finding a loving partner is the solution to your problems? I hope not.

So make sure you don't discuss these things in your profile. The bottom line is to let others reflect on how attractive, interesting, and memorable you are. If you are so angry or depressed that these feelings spill over into your profile, you might want to take more time to heal before you try online dating. Those negative feelings will eventually seep out and destroy any relationship you develop—online or offline.

Some people give surface answers or cryptic, three-word responses in their profiles. You might just as well insert a grunt or a stick-figure drawing. Other profiles reek of poor cyberstyle because they are full of spelling and grammar mistakes. If you want to waste your time and money, then dismiss the importance of creating a compelling profile.

Here are a few opening lines to avoid:

- "I hate talking about myself..." (Wait until you feel better about yourself and can find something to say.)
- "I never know how to begin..." (Try saying something that's more interesting than this.)
- "I don't know what else to say..." (Just end your profile and don't ramble.)
- "I hate this! How can you give a full description of yourself in such a short space?" (Yeah, and negative people are *so* attractive!)
- "I'll fill this out later..." (Are we supposed to wait around for you?)

If you're adamant about moving forward but don't feel you have enough to say, just cover the essentials, be positive in your statements, and include something that shows your personality and interests. Incorporate your answers to the questions about your spiritual life in chapter 2, your descriptions of your goals and interests in chapter 3, and information from the Profile Helper later in this chapter.

Think about it this way. Most singles have little trouble describing their ideal match in great detail—sometimes *way too much* detail. Does a woman really need to have hair of a certain color, or does a man have to earn more than $50,000 annually? But look at the self-description in some of those same profiles. You might get three or four sentences telling you about the person compared to an encyclopedia on the qualities that he or she is seeking in a partner. Don't go there. The profile is your cyber-space version of you, not a fast-food order.

Kelli, a kindergarten teacher who is married to a man she met online, waded through more boring profiles than she cares to remember. "After you've been online for a while, all the profiles sound the same," she recalls. "Most say they are laid-back, down-to-earth guys who hate drama and are looking for a fit, attractive Christian girl who is comfortable dressing up in an evening gown and in blue jeans, as well as someone who loves all the sports they like and will be their Proverbs 31 woman and will know how to allow them to be real men. I would skip over those profiles, wondering who these guys *really* are. They don't give me any positive or interesting reasons to remember them, let alone contact them. Tell me why I should stop looking and want to be with you. Don't just tell me all about what *you* want."

Profiles on Life Support

Do yourself a big favor and avoid the leading killers of online profiles:

Poor spelling and grammar. Maybe spelling and grammar are not important to *you,* but think about those you are trying to attract. Will they want to correspond with a semiliterate or sloppy person? Men, listen up. Spelling and grammar issues matter to women. When you send an e-mail riddled with spelling and grammar errors, it's the same as if you had shown up for a date wearing a wrinkled, sloppy, smelly shirt. If you have trouble with spelling and grammar, compose your profile responses and then run the spelling and grammar checks. You can cut and paste the cleaned-up file to your profile. Some sites offer online spell checkers. There are free spell checkers online as well. If you type in the keywords "spell check" and "online," the free online spell checkers should pop up.

Not answering open-ended questions fully. Men outnumber women on the Internet, so men especially need to make an extra effort to stand out from the crowd. If a man doesn't give a woman enough information to want to get to know him, she will simply move on to the next thousand guys who posted more memorable profiles.

Pursue your matches using all the tools at your disposal. Try hard to describe yourself. And *do not* put in your profile: "I don't have time to finish this now but will do so later." If you don't have time to fill out your profile, then wait for a better time. Incomplete profiles give the impression that you're lazy or just don't care.

Boring, cliché-ridden, sappy, or pretentious profiles. It takes no imagination to be sappy, to rely on clichés, or to state the obvious. That's just boring, and it makes you seem as if you have no personality. Boring profiles are too general and offer no insights into one's personality. There is no wit or creativity. Too many of them simply restate vital statistics: age, weight, height, body type, job, and other demographic data. Try this one on for size:

I'm not much on describing myself!!! All I can say is that you
won't be disappointed. I am thirty-four, yet I look at least seven
years younger than I am. —Lonely in GA

Lonely down in Georgia might not remain in Georgia, but we can bet he'll stay lonely. Merely saying that a person won't be disappointed is no reason to believe it. He also listed himself as thirty-four, so why is looking seven years younger so important? Usually people over fifty make statements like this, so perhaps Lonely is thirty-four, looks fifty, and might pass for forty-three (seven years younger). Don't know; don't care. This is the attitude that people will take if you force them to think too much about why you wrote something in your profile.

To avoid being boring, use vivid, colorful words. Avoid the tried and overused. Men and women each have their own clichés. So before you post your profile, screen it for sappiness and cliché abuse. Here are some common clichés:

Common Male Profile Clichés
- "I'm a down-to-earth guy."
- "I am a hopeless romantic."
- "Chivalry is not dead."
- "I'm a laid-back individual."
- "I'm looking for a Proverbs-31 wife."

Common Female Profile Clichés
- "I'm looking for a good, honest Christian man."
- "I am low maintenance."
- "I am outgoing."
- "Looking for someone who puts God first."
- "I'm a positive, upbeat person."

Swear off sappiness. If you think you're a poet, keep it to yourself. There are way too many Internet Casanovas who use poetry and sap to try to woo naive women. Resist the urge to send out stuff like this: "I'm in search of true love, the one to spend my forever with. / I'm in search of a dream, to know what it means to actually be happy. / I want to know that when I close my eyes and open them in the morning that my dream will not be over, only that it will continue forever."[1] Are you gagging yet? Sending "poetry" such as this communicates that (1) the person is out of touch with reality, or (2) he or she is desperate.

The pretentious profile. Christians usually understand the concept of modesty, but they can come across as pretentious, conceited, or too perfect. Please, spare us. Typically, overt pretentiousness on secular online dating sites comes from people who brag about being pilots, architects, lawyers, investors who made it big, and other high-status professionals with money and impressive accomplishments.

> I am a people-pleaser who loves to please, pamper, and spoil!!!—I decided to wait until I was successful and financially independent to marry and raise a family. As a mature Christian, I desire a Christian Lady. I love to cook, clean house, cuddle, snuggle, and kiss. I am extremely handsome and have worked as a model and actor and have owned my own film company. Now I am the vice president of an Oil and Gas company. Serious inquiries only. Thank you. —Your Final Choice

I didn't make this one up. It came from a popular online dating site. Final Choice sees himself as quite a catch and doesn't mind telling us all about it—in a smug sort of way. It may be true that he's been a model and actor and film company owner *and* the vice president of an oil and gas company, but it's way over the top. It makes him come across as pretentious and unattractive. (Who knows? Maybe he was only a hand model.) And the talk about how he loves to "please, pamper, and spoil" combined with the fact that he loves to "cook, clean house, cuddle, snuggle, and kiss" demands that we be either gullible or unexplainably willing to join him in his fantasy world.

Just to be even-handed, I'll include a pretentious posting from a woman:

> Hi there, where do I begin? Well, I'll start with my job. I work at NASA as a flight controller for the shuttle program. That means I work in the Mission Control Center during space shuttle missions. It's a great job and I absolutely love it. Currently, however, I'm temporarily working as a liaison between NASA and the Russian Space Agency. Incredible, right? I can't wait to share this exciting life with someone special. God is so good to me and during my time in Russia for my job, I have volunteered for several mission trips to more remote areas. I'm looking for someone who wants to share this adventure with me. —Single in Space

Before you surrender to the gag reflex, let me tell you that I can vouch for Single in Space because I know her. She may not have a good grasp on how she's coming across to others, but she *is* a wonderful person. Her ad, however, would scare off most men. She comes across as being too into herself and maybe just a tad too good to be true. If this were a man's profile, many women would assume it's just a guy using a worn-out pickup line—"Want to fly to the moon, baby?" The problem with people who have fabulous careers is that they come across as sounding superior if they talk about it too much. People tend to want to marry a regular human being, not Neil Armstrong or Sally Ride.

On Christian sites, pretentiousness can take a different course, and people can tend to come across as superpious or too holy. These are the people who quote in their profile every Bible verse they know. Instead of talking like normal people when you chat with them, they fill their comments with Christian jargon and make sure you know they toe the Christian line. They may be the most sincere people out there, but online they come across as pretentious and judgmental.

So hold back on the career enthusiasm, zealous missionary talk, and Bible quoting until you really get to know a person. That way, he or she will hear the sincerity of your heart and won't mistake you for a self-centered (albeit pious) egotist.

FIRST AID FOR THE LIMPING PROFILE

Let's write a profile that really works. First, be specific. If you love sports, talk about which sports you love and why. You love to travel? Where do you like to go? You say you love music? Mozart or Metallica? Huge difference. Read books? Which authors? Perhaps your definition of *the classics* includes Mark Twain, while someone you are pursuing thinks *classic* refers to a hard-to-find Star Wars comic book. Remember, the goal of a profile is to present yourself as attractive, interesting, and memorable. Millions of singles love music, reading, sports, and/or travel. But few singles write specifically enough for someone reading their profile to make a meaningful connection with them.

To produce a compelling profile, gather your thoughts about yourself and your interests before you start writing. Use the Profile Helper below to get your thoughts organized and on paper.

Profile Helper

1. Where are you from, and what city do you live in now?

2. What do you do for a living? What is satisfying about your job? (Be positive.)

3. How long have you been a Christian? Why or how did you decide to follow Christ?

4. Where do you see yourself in five years?

5. How would you describe your sense of humor—dry, sarcastic, slapstick? What made you laugh out loud recently?

6. What CD is currently in your player? How does this CD reflect your musical tastes?

7. What was the last movie you really enjoyed, and why did you enjoy it so much?

8. What was the last book you read? Why did you like it?

9. Where was the last place you traveled? What did you enjoy about the trip?

10. Where do you dream about traveling in the future, and why?

11. What are the three things you enjoy most about life? Why?

12. What three words would your family and friends (not your mother) use to describe you? (Remember, you're being positive.)

13. Describe the best type of date you've ever had. Why was it the best? (Note where you went, what you did, etc., but don't describe the person you were dating.)

14. How would you describe your current relationship with God? How close are you to Him? How would you evaluate your spiritual vitality?

15. What are the top three things you're passionate about—the things that get you debating, reflecting, questioning, or lost in conversation? What prompts you to volunteer for a cause?

16. What do you want to accomplish with your profile? Are you looking for friends, a spouse or other long-term relationship, pen pals, e-mail buddies, conversation, or support?

Once you have written down your responses, edit them so they flow together and tell a story of who you are. It's good to have a long self-description at this point. You can edit it later. Using the Profile Helper will enable you to focus on revealing who you are and why *you* are someone worth finding. Since you don't want to write a book, keep editing your self-description until every sentence succinctly describes who you are.

The final step is to describe your ideal match. Go back to chapter 5 and review your Essential Qualities Matrix. Choose your top five to seven nonnegotiable attributes in a match and your top two or three optional but preferred attributes. You have to be specific enough to alert people that your nonnegotiable attributes are truly essential. Many people find that after they get to know someone and even fall in love, some of their nonnegotiables are no longer applicable. What seems like a deal breaker now could easily become a nonissue if you meet the right person. If, however, you have been burned or if you have such strong convictions that nonnegotiable preferences are just that, then make that clear. Leave no doubt about whom you are seeking.

Get Honest, *Real* Honest

The biggest complaint among online daters is that people tend to be less than honest about themselves. It's tempting to embellish or minimize even the straightforward descriptions in a profile. Although Christian sites have fewer dishonest members, many Christians have deluded themselves into thinking that their half-truths are not lies—perhaps thinking that cyberspace has different rules. Go figure. Bait and switch is just as unethical in cyberspace as it is in the real world. And Scripture requires us to be completely truthful (see Colossians 3:9-10). Now is not the time to start bending biblical rules for how we are to relate to one another.

"I fell hard for this Christian lady, and when it was clear that we both felt deeply for each other, I wanted to move to an offline relationship," says Miguel, a man in his early forties. "She said she wasn't ready, so I backed off. A month went by and we were still having our usual deep conversations, and I couldn't take it anymore. I had to see her. But it was excuse after excuse.

"She finally agreed to meet me, and I was shocked that she was much heavier than her picture. She said she was working out to lose the weight. I was hurt that she wasn't honest with me. I couldn't shake feeling that if she lied to me about this, what else was she lying about? So just be honest, and if someone doesn't like you for you, then he wasn't meant for you anyway."

To help keep yourself honest, pretend that you and your online match will meet in person *tomorrow*. If you are overweight and are slimming down, you can't lose weight overnight. If you are going bald, you won't find a good toupee or hair transplant in twenty-four hours. (And don't even think about using spray-on hair!) If you're out of work, you won't become a junior executive by this time tomorrow. Being less than truthful online will undermine your success. The fear of being discovered and then rejected will prevent you from becoming closer in your relationship.

PROFILE EVALUATOR

Now that you've completed your profile, look at it closely to see how you're coming across. Ask a close friend or family member to give you an impartial assessment. The Profile Evaluator below will help you ensure that your profile is doing its job.

Profile Evaluator

1. Are you being honest about everything you have included? Have you avoided embellishments and half-truths? If you haven't been honest or find you've been telling half-truths, why do you think you acted this way? What, if anything, are you trying to hide about yourself?

2. Is the tone of your profile positive and upbeat? If not, ask yourself if you are angry, frustrated, afraid, or depressed. What can you do to change the tone?

3. Have you included humor and cleverness? If so, do you honestly believe that people who don't know you will find your humor attractive? If not, what can you do to incorporate these qualities into your profile?

4. Are there any spelling or grammar errors in your profile? If so, what can you do to ensure an error-free profile?

5. Have you avoided using all caps or all lowercase letters in your message? If not, why do you think you wrote this way? Do you understand how some people who read your message may see you as lazy or angry?

6. Does your profile make sense, and does your story have good flow? If not, why doesn't your writing make sense? Were you rushing or under stress? What can you do to improve in these areas?

7. Can a stranger tell that you love the Lord and are a follower of Christ? If not, why are you not reflecting the joy of the Lord? Are you experiencing some spiritual setbacks right now?

8. Have you avoided generalizations? Have you described your interests in detail? In what ways can you be more descriptive in your profile and reveal more about your personality?

9. Did you include anything that makes your profile memorable, such as creativity, wit, or something you are passionate about? If not, why do you think you are having a hard time identifying something memorable to include? What can you do to make some positive changes in this area and live a fuller and richer life in Christ?

10. Are you coming across as too preachy, too perfect, or otherwise unapproachable? How can you reflect maturity in Christ without coming across as "holier than thou"?

11. When describing your ideal match, do you seem too rigid, unrealistic, or smug? In what ways are you being naive, unrealistic, or too overbearing in describing your ideal match? What can you do to fix this problem?

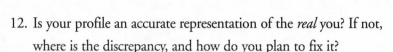

12. Is your profile an accurate representation of the *real* you? If not, where is the discrepancy, and how do you plan to fix it?

Profile Headlines

You need added creativity for the final act. Create a catchy headline that announces to the cyberworld that you are worth a person's time and attention. Most profile headlines are boring, sappy, or cliché-ridden, so avoid the top ten headlines (as well as their variations):

- SCM ISO SCF—Single Christian Male in search of Single Christian Female. (So what else is new?)
- Hi. (Bye. Moving right along.)
- Chivalry is not dead. (Yeah, but statements like this should be.)
- Seeking my soul mate. (Aren't we all?)
- Laid-back guy searching for an attractive Christian woman. (A little too laid-back to think of something new to say?)
- Lonely, divorced woman in search of love again. (Here we go again with that lonely thing.)
- Prince seeking his princess; king seeking his queen. (I bet you're also dying to lay some sappy poetry on me.)
- Handsome/beautiful Christian man/woman in search of... (A little pretentious here, aren't we?)
- Christian woman in search of Man of God. (Blah, blah, blah.)
- Looking for Mr./Ms. Right. (Really? I was sure you were holding out for Mr./Ms. Wrong.)

Successful online dating requires a healthy dose of creativity so you will stand out from the crowd. You will notice right away that most people's profiles start looking and sounding the same. So stretch yourself when writing your headline. Think in terms of attractive, interesting, and memorable. The following headline is the most interesting I've seen in a while: "Adam in Search of His Missing Rib."

Okay, so the guy's name is probably Stan. He's taking poetic license to stand out. Or maybe he's just making the point that he's serious about relationships. Call it sappy if you want, but it's not preachy, pushy, or pious. Actually, when I saw this headline, my first thought was, *Gross!*—which does not fit the "attractive" requirement (see above). However, I was compelled to at least look at the profile to learn more about this man. Getting someone to read your profile is what your headline should accomplish.

Say something fresh, creative, clever, and even funny. Remember, everyone's taste is different, so do something that reflects you in the best light, and if someone is attracted by your creativity, then you have been successful. Some headlines that caught my eye recently were "Knight in Slightly Rusty Armor" and "Are You the Eve for This Steve?"

Even if it's not hilarious, it might just make someone look more closely.

Seven

Make a Connection That Matters

How to Separate the Maybes from the No-Ways

When you date others online, you are greatly expanding the universe of potential partners. What a contrast to the limited number of potential partners you meet when you attend singles' events at church or a party at a friend's house. Not only are you greatly enlarging the pool of potential dates when you date online, but you are also doing so without the visual clues that we all rely on in person-to-person interaction. You can't watch the other person's face to gauge whether he or she is bored, distracted, or paying attention. Neither can you read the person's body language to see if he or she is relaxed or uptight. When you communicate on the Internet, you miss out on much of the visual data that is useful in making an assessment of the other person.

In the absence of visual clues, what can you do to make accurate assessments of those you meet on the Internet? And how can you be discerning about a person's forthrightness and whether he or she fits the qualities you're seeking?

If you want to know the best way to screen the e-mails of those who respond to your profile, then keep reading. If you're curious about the best way to make first contact with someone whose profile interests you, this chapter is for you. If you want to encourage a greater number of responses to your initial e-mail contacts with other singles, read on. Wondering what to ask or talk about in your first few e-mail conversations? Yep, it's in this chapter. You will also learn what you should look for as you search profiles, send e-mail introductions, and respond to e-mails from those who are intrigued by your profile.

Read on to discover the art of making meaningful contact with other singles online.

The Right Start

Kendra is an executive assistant who remembers well the uncertainty she felt when she began dating online.

"It took me forever, but I finished my profile and got my picture uploaded. Then I froze big time," she says. "I didn't know what to do next. Should I just wait for responses, or was I to start searching other profiles? And there were so many profiles. How could I search without being at my computer all night? It can get on your nerves after a while because it eats up all your time."

Kendra's observations summarize the frustration and indecision that many encounter with online dating. It's not always clear how to proceed, and it's really, *really* time consuming. You can actively search for matches yourself by sorting profiles. This gives you more control, but make sure to set aside plenty of time for it. Or you can sit back and wait for others to respond to your profile. This approach consumes far less of your time, but you might be left waiting awhile. Or if you're using a true matchmaker site, you simply wait for computer matches to be sent to you.

If you choose to search profiles and send e-mails introducing yourself, be prepared for a modest rate of response. Many online dating sites tell men they should be happy with a 1 percent response rate to their e-mail introductions. A similar rate may apply to women dating online. Your response rate may improve, though, if you make sure your e-mail introduction, profile, and pictures are attractive, interesting, and memorable. If you choose to wait for a matchmaker site to send you matches, you may have to wait even longer for responses, depending on your preferences and the attributes you are seeking in a match. The most hands-off approach is to simply post your profile and then wait to see who responds. To succeed with this approach, make sure your profile is extremely compelling and memorable. You need to stand out from the crowd of thousands.

No matter which strategy you choose, be patient and persistent. You never know when the right person will join an online dating service or find the time to send that first e-mail introduction.

STAGES OF ONLINE RELATIONSHIPS

Relationships that develop online tend to follow a predictable sequence. Although there are some variations, online relationships tend to progress (or end) in this order:

Stage 1: Initial attraction. After searching profiles or looking at the profile of someone who has sent you an e-mail, you're interested enough to want to know more.

Stage 2: First contact. You send an initial e-mail or instant message introducing yourself. Or you invite someone to join you in a private chat room.

Stage 3: First telephone call or voice-chat meeting. You want to hear the other person's voice, so you arrange for a phone conversation or a voice-chat meeting. This stage can last for couple of days or a few months, depending on how quickly the couple's attraction deepens and how soon they wish to move on to stage 4. Distance also plays a part in the timing of the next stage.

Stage 4: First in-person meeting. Thanks to the widespread use of Web cams, people who are dating online can see each other long before they meet in person. Although Web cam technology is getting better, body language and other nonverbal communication are still less clearly seen through Web cams than in real life. The use of Web cams in general tends to signal more intimacy in the relationship; however, many people skip straight to Web cam or video chats in place of voice chats or telephone conversations.

Then there is the first nonvirtual face-to-face meeting, which signals a huge step forward in the relationship. Again, some people prefer to skip stage 3 and, after a few e-mails or chat sessions, go straight to a face-to-face meeting. If they live relatively nearby, that is often the case.

Stage 5: The turning point. This involves a decision to continue the relationship or break up. After you meet in person, you need to decide whether to keep things moving ahead. Sometimes individuals will break off the relationship earlier. It can happen during any stage. (For a detailed discussion of breaking off an online relationship, see chapter 8.)

Stage 6: Exclusivity. This stage can come much earlier in the sequence. During this stage both people take their profiles off the Web and stop communicating with other potential matches. Problems occur when the two parties don't agree on what stage their relationship is in. Sometimes one person thinks they're exclusive, but the other is still contacting other matches. It's important to settle on your shared understanding of where the relationship is at.

WHO'S WORTH YOUR TIME?

Now you have a clear understanding not only of yourself but also of the person you are hoping to find. However, not all of the things you are looking for in another person will be reflected in the profiles you view. So you'll have to determine whether the profile includes enough information for you to make contact with the person so you can gather more information.

To maximize your time online, develop a system to use in sorting your contacts and interactions with potential matches. Some online daters divide their contacts into three folders: (1) people I want to contact, (2) people I might want to get to know, and (3) people I don't want to pursue further. But how do you sort the Yes, No, and Maybe files?

It's best to rely on objective criteria for determining whom you will share your heart with online. There are too many people who manipulate the emotions of others, so don't fall victim to someone who might simply lead you on. Also, objective criteria will keep you from assuming that your first emotion, or your strongest emotion, is necessarily the one you should follow. You can't always trust your gut reaction or your initial attraction to a person (see Proverbs 19:2-3). Your emotional reactions to e-mail or instant messages are important to pay attention to, but sometimes they can lead you off track. Without a more objective system, you might screen out someone who really is a good match, or you could allow a relationship to develop with someone who is not compatible with you.

To screen effectively, first commit to memory your preferences for your ideal match. Size up each potential match who appeals to you in relation to how closely he or she fits your ideal. Sure, the person may not fit all your preferences, but if he or she lacks many of your essential attributes, then you may have to take a pass. As you screen people, you will also be forced to refine the list of traits that you previously thought were mandatory.

If you find yourself falling for someone who is eloquent and romantic but does not closely fit your ideal match, stop and take a deep breath. Then take a few more. Then ask yourself,

- Are the qualities I listed as nonnegotiable truly mandatory for my ideal mate? Do they still accurately reflect who I am looking for?
- Am I casting aside my predetermined list of essential qualities so I can pursue a person who doesn't possess enough of the required traits?

The sample comparison table on page 127 was filled out by Trina, a Miami waitress. The table shows that David has many of the qualities Trina is seeking, but she needs to probe more deeply into the Maybe and Flag areas. Create a table similar to Trina's as a way to protect yourself from being swept away by your emotions when you are evaluating a match. List all of your essential traits first, and then list the optional ones. If you're feeling strong emotions toward a match, compare him or her with your own traits as well as those you are looking for in an ideal match (review your Essential Qualities Matrix in chapter 5).

You can also use an online journal, with your screening criteria filled in, to record the progress you make with your matches. As the relationship progresses and you discuss issues, views, beliefs, and traits with the other person, fill in your comparison checklist. Out of all the attributes that you deem important, count how many desired attributes the potential match possesses.

Tommy, a twenty-eight-year-old counselor from Atlanta, dated online for a year. He is now married to Jessica, a match he met online. He reflects on what he learned: "The good thing about going online is that I learned so much about myself and what I really wanted in a wife. At first, I was strict about what type of woman I was attracted to. I thought I could only be attracted to slender women, but then I met Jessica.... She and I were compatible on all the other things I wanted in a wife. We had the best time online, and then on the phone. When I saw her, I saw that she wasn't a small woman...but she was beautiful. She suited me well."

Criteria	Trina	My Ideal Match	Person's Name: David	Is There a Match?
ESSENTIAL TRAITS				
Age	33	30–45	42	Yes
Body Type	Athletic	Slender, athletic, a few extra pounds	Athletic	Yes
Political Affiliation	Conservative Republican	Conservative	Conservative	Yes
Religious Affiliation	Southern Baptist	Southern Baptist	Nondenominational	Flag
Marital Status	Single, never married	Single, never married, widowed, or divorced (depends)	Divorced	Maybe, but need to know more
Number of Children	None	None	2, living away from home	Maybe
OPTIONAL TRAITS				
Pets	Dalmatian	Dog lover	No pets, allergic	Flag
Occupation	Waitress	Anything other than police officer	Minister	Maybe
Total Matches: 6 matches or possible matches out of 8 possible matches				

Making an Initial Contact

There are two ways you can make first contact: (1) you find a profile that is appealing, and you decide to send an e-mail to the person, or (2) you receive an e-mail from someone who seems interesting and attractive, and you decide to respond. Either way, what do you say in your first e-mail?

If you are initiating first contact in response to a profile you found interesting, you may find that many people won't accept instant messages from you because you're a stranger. Most people want time to evaluate whether they want to talk to you. An instant message can seem pushy.

Instead, send an e-mail that says enough to make the other person want to know more and start talking with you. Never leave the subject line blank. You need to be creative because your e-mail will land in a full in-box. Your subject line needs to be just as memorable as the headline on your profile. Try a variation of your profile headline or mention something from the person's profile. Avoid "Hi there" and "What's up?"

Want to avoid sending e-mails that bomb? Avoid these top seven e-mail-introduction mistakes.

1. Using a form letter. I know you're busy and get tired of being creative and personalizing each e-mail, especially when the other person never responds. But here's the bottom line: People react negatively to form letters. "How can they tell?" you ask. It's easy: Form letters, even the "creative" ones, tend to be a person's profile in e-mail form. It talks only about the person sending the e-mail:

Hello,

I am a thirty-five-year-old lawyer living in Los Angeles. I am a prosecutor and have been one for the last three years. I have spent

quite a bit of my time getting ahead and found myself brought to
my knees when I got in a terrible accident and thought I would
die. Before the accident, I had a lousy relationship with God. I'm
fine now, but lonely and want to share my life with someone special. I do not have much time to go out and meet new people. I
work long hours and teach at my church.

I am six feet tall and could stand to lose a few pounds, but I
don't have too much hanging off my belt. I have attached a pic so
you can see. Now to my heart. I have been in Christ for fifteen
years, but not all of those years was I a strong Christian. I have a
dry sense of humor and enjoy reading Christian fiction and inspi-
rational books. I hate television and the movies. I do love to travel
but don't really want to travel much outside of the U.S. I'm not
into foreign foods too much.

I love all sports. Hey, I'm a man, so sue me.☺ I especially love
any kind of outdoor sport and would love to share that with someone special. I am looking for a strong Christian woman who is
ready to settle down. I am looking for a woman who takes care of
her mind, body, and spirit. If you are interested, send me an e-mail
and we can go from there.

Blessings,

Jonathan

Jonathan sent this e-mail to hundreds of women and received very
few responses. He wondered why, since the e-mail paints a picture of a
pretty decent guy. And it's not a badly written e-mail. The problem is that
it's generic. It sounds just like his profile. Even worse, it sounds like a mass
mailing to any and all women. This is online dating spam, and most savvy
online daters will delete these e-mails. Everyone wants to feel special, but

it's hard to feel that way when the other person talks only about himself or herself.

You need to personalize your e-mails for each person you contact. Show the person that you read his or her profile. Mention something from the person's profile or e-mail that grabbed your attention. Talk about some of the things you have in common. Let the person know why you decided to send an e-mail. Don't just spam people with your generic introduction in hopes that someone—please, anyone—will respond. If you're a member of more than one singles dating service, you could end up sending the same form letter to the same person under different screen names.

2. Sending overly short e-mails. "Hi, I'm Kathy and I liked your ad. If you are interested, let's talk." Kathy is most likely a fine person, but she doesn't give the e-mail recipient enough information to spark an interest. So Kathy, get a little energy and take some initiative. Don't make the other person do all the work.

You need to give people a reason to want to get to know you. Make it hard for recipients to delete your message.

3. Sending an inappropriately personal or offensive e-mail. Consider this example of a first e-mail that is inappropriately personal and should never leave your outbox:

Hi, I liked your profile. I'm glad to know you have been in Christ for so long. Reading that warmed my heart. I see that you have never been married. Neither have I. I'm also pleased to see that you do not have any children. I don't have children either. Now, if you are a virgin, let me know so that we can get to know each other better.

I look forward to talking to you.

Benny

Benny, Benny, Benny. Do I really need to explain this? No one, especially Christians, should talk about anything sexual in an e-mail like this—unless you don't want a response. Asking if a person is a virgin in an e-mail is way too personal.[1] Would you ask this question if you met the person face to face? If you would, then you need to stop dating altogether and develop some social skills.

If finding someone who is a virgin is your top, nonnegotiable requirement, then get to know the person much better and then *wait*. There will be a right time to ask the question after you've met in person, have dated, and have talked seriously about marriage. In fact, it's best to ask this question in the presence of a minister, mentor, or Christian counselor.

4. Asking for a picture and that's it. "Hi, I saw your ad. Can you send me two current pics of yourself right away? Looking forward to seeing you soon." —Bruce

Bruce, do you realize how shallow this sounds? Many people, especially men, want to get a sense of what a person looks like right away. As we discussed earlier, many people use online dating like an introduction service and do not wish to spend too much time online developing a relationship. Instead, they prefer to determine if there is an initial attraction so they can move the relationship offline. Others make physical attraction their top nonnegotiable trait in a potential match, so they prefer not to spend time with anyone who might fall short of their standard later on. Finally, some online daters request a photo so they can more easily bond with the other person, rather than using it to screen out people whose looks don't meet their expectations.

Regardless of your reasons for wanting a picture, there are ways to ask that won't turn off the other person. By asking for a picture and saying nothing else, you give the impression that you found the person's profile (his or her heart) attractive enough to initiate contact, but you are putting off talking to the person until you get a good look at him or her.

5. *Sending a negative message.* It's pretty hard to attract a person you've insulted in your first e-mail. Take a look at this example of what not to say:

> Hi, I'm Cindy and wanted to say that you have a funny profile. I laughed really hard. Thank you for the biggest smile I had all day. I have a stressful job and really should look for another one because it's sad when I have to read an ad on a dating site to give me my best laugh all day—maybe all week. Anyway, we have a lot in common and I just wanted to say hi, although I know you like *Star Wars* movies. I think Christians have no business watching those types of movies. You can't really serve two masters.
> Hope to talk to you soon.
> Cindy

Who knows where Cindy's head is? Is the guy she contacted funny and charming, or is he a backsliding Christian because he enjoys *Star Wars*? You can't tell what she's trying to accomplish here.

I wouldn't hold my breath waiting for a response, girlfriend. Assuming you weren't mocking this poor guy, you started out great. Your note is positive, personal, and complimentary for a few sentences. But you start to falter when you gripe about your stressful job. And then the *Star Wars* dig. C'mon.

Let's all learn from Cindy. Talking about your last relationship, griping about your job or church, and bringing up anything negative or stressful in your life should be kept out of your first contact. Even at that, Cindy probably could have gotten away with a small work-related complaint because of her prior compliment on the guy's profile. But then she got herself disqualified when she insulted his taste in movies and questioned his Christian commitment. If Cindy had such a strong objection to his choice in movies, then why bother sending an e-mail?

6. *Sending a disingenuous or worn-out pickup line.* The following first-contact message fails in every way. The goal is not to make someone laugh at you or gag.

> Dear Sister,
> I read your profile, and I prayed hard before e-mailing you. I can't believe you are still single. God is blessing me by having a chance with you. Has anyone told you that your profile exudes the aroma of Christ? I know deep down inside that you would make an excellent Proverbs 31 wife. If you want to talk further, let me know.
> Steve

Give Steve an award for mixing metaphors and muddling Scripture. It's hard to know where to start with a critique. Everything about this e-mail is wrong. There is no way from reading a profile that Steve could know this woman would make even a halfway decent friend, let alone a great wife. He sent this form-letter e-mail to several women who all groaned at the aroma-of-Christ reference. This sad attempt at making a good impression gives Steve's e-mail a certain aroma, but not a good one. The women who received this e-mail sniffed out a moldy pickup line. Steve may be the sweetest man around, but his e-mail turns women sour.

7. *Sending an overly romantic and sappy e-mail.* The following e-mail should put all the online poets out there on notice. Stuff like this doesn't work for first contact.

My dearest darling,

When I saw your picture, I knew that God had revealed to me the woman whom *He* created for me to be my soul mate. Your warm, beautiful, captivating smile reminds me of the heavenly sky illuminated by the crescent moon that shines upon God's beautiful earth and blesses it with the warm rays of light. Your smile lights up my heart and soul. I have dreamed of a strong Christian woman like you, and you are my beloved and I am yours.... I am ready to share all of my life with my beloved, and I know she will rise up in the morning and go to bed at night to consider herself blessed indeed.... Can you handle long walks by the beach on moonlit nights? How about long, romantic dinners as we share our hearts and soul with each other forever? Are you ready for an adventure, my beloved? If so, please let me know. You will not be disappointed. I promise.

Tony

I took pity on you and edited Tony's note. Actually, I was taking pity on myself. Enough already.

Tony is a hopeless romantic and doesn't realize that he's sent a stinker of an e-mail. Sending out overly romantic or sappy first e-mails tends to backfire. Men think women want to see their romantic and sensitive side, so they try to get in touch with the poet within. The problem with this e-mail is not just that it's sappy. The bigger issue is that it's *way* too premature. Women immediately see through e-mails like this one. Tony's a stranger, after all. He can't possibly know all of this just by looking at a photo on the Internet.

If you are dying to display your romantic side, wait until you have established a relationship. Make sure the other person feels strongly about you and will welcome your overtures. Otherwise you'll simply prove that you're a really bad poet—and an insincere one at that.

The Successful First E-Mail

You'll increase your chances for success if you keep a few simple e-mail guidelines in mind. In addition to keeping your first e-mail positive, interesting, and memorable, keep in mind seven things you should do:

1. Make it clear that you have read the person's profile and his or her description of an ideal match. Indicate how you fit the person's desired match, if only in part.
2. Ask a few questions that show that you want to know more about the person.
3. Make sure to end your e-mail with a warm and positive thought that lets the person know you wish them well regardless of whether he or she chooses to respond. It can be as simple as "Wishing you the best" or "May God bless you in your search." Although these phrases can be overused and trite, the goal is to bless the other person.
4. Politely ask the person to respond, even if he or she does not want to continue corresponding. Let the person know that your world will not collapse if you learn that he or she isn't interested.
5. Tell only part of your story so you can keep some interesting information for future conversations. A two- or three-page introductory e-mail is overkill.
6. Make sure you include some wit and creativity. However, if you find in other contexts that others don't appreciate your quirky sense of humor, keep it under wraps for now.
7. Always check your spelling and grammar before you hit the Send button.

Not Getting a Response?

What should you do if you receive too few e-mails in response to your introduction? Many people come to online dating thinking that once they enlarge their social network, they'll find plenty of promising matches. They post their profile expecting their in-box to be full by the end of the week. However, many singles end up learning this hard lesson: Even among millions of people online, you still might not find someone you will date, let alone marry.

Why wouldn't everyone eventually find someone? Until more Christians post their profiles, those with less than ideal personal circumstances are still at a disadvantage online. People who currently receive fewer responses include:

- people who are overweight or unattractive by our culture's standards
- people who have a disability, chronic illness, or any disfigurement
- those older than fifty
- those with dependent children living at home
- members of an ethnic minority
- those belonging to a small denomination
- those who live in a smaller city or a rural area

If you fit any of these categories, it doesn't mean you won't be successful online. Online dating tends to level the playing field, allowing others to get to know your heart and soul without the initial distractions of physical appearance or personal limitations. People who fall into any of these categories will naturally feel that Christians should transcend the world's standards in their search for a spouse. Unfortunately, this ideal is not the case for everyone who dates online. It may take you awhile to find someone who can see your heart first, so pray for patience and ask God to protect your heart.

Help! I'm Getting Too Much E-Mail

Maybe this doesn't sound like a problem, but it is. Why would anyone object to receiving *too much* correspondence? The excitement of having a full mailbox wears off as you begin sorting the e-mail only to discover that most of the people are nothing like your ideal match. So what do you do?

Your first step is to analyze the responses you're receiving. If an overwhelming number of responses come from people who are unlike your ideal match, or if you are getting too many e-mails from pornographers or scary people, take immediate action. Revise your profile to specify and highlight the qualities your ideal match must have. And make sure your photo, profile, and screen name don't signal that you're looking for anything other than an honorable Christian relationship. If you address those concerns and still receive too much inappropriate e-mail, then reconsider the Web sites you are using. Are the unwanted e-mails coming from one particular site?

Answering those questions and correcting any unintentional messages you may be sending should reduce the number of unwanted e-mails. Women might still receive a fair amount of unwanted e-mail because men tend to send form letters to large numbers of women in the off chance that someone might respond.

But what if you are receiving too many e-mails from people who match your ideal? Then brace yourself for a time-consuming screening process as you whittle down your in-box to those who most closely fit your ideal match.

Eight

Breaking Up Is Still Hard to Do

How to Make the Best of Ending a Relationship

Fifteen years ago single adults would not have been able to imagine having access to such a vast pool of potential matches. Online dating truly is a worldwide search.

But while your pool of potential dating partners may expand greatly when you date online, you may end up cutting off more relationships than you would if you were dating offline. You may be able to gather more information about a larger number of potential matches, but your ability to make an accurate judgment about a match's suitability is more limited than it is offline. For example, you can't observe how your match interacts with others, and chances are slim that you and your match know any of the same people. Also, as discussed in previous chapters, you don't have the benefit of nonverbal communication signals. In the absence of conventional social cues, you have to make decisions based largely on the information the other person provides. Once you gather enough information to make an informed decision, you will probably end up rejecting many would-be dates. And you will likely end up being rejected by many. Neither is easy.

When you decide it's time to reject an interested party, you need to know the best way to word a rejection so it will inflict the least amount of damage to the other person's self-confidence. Rejection is particularly painful and problematic during the last three stages of an online dating relationship. Since you have been getting to know each other through the first three stages, your decision to end the relationship later in the process can generate more inner conflict for you. Likewise, it can cause more pain for the other person. So proceed with mercy and compassion.

How do you prepare for rejecting someone and being rejected? And how can you know it's the right time to end a relationship? In this chapter we'll explore the answers to these questions. But first, here's a recap of the stages of an online relationship:

- *Stage 1*—Initial attraction, sparked by reading an online personal ad or profile or by reading an e-mail sent by someone who read your profile.
- *Stage 2*—First contact is made by sending an introductory e-mail.
- *Stage 3*—First telephone call or voice-chat meeting.
- *Stage 4*—First in-person meeting.
- *Stage 5*—The turning point, after meeting face to face, which involves a decision to continue or break up.
- *Stage 6*—Exclusivity in developing just this relationship.

A Closer Look at Rejection

How can we minimize the chances of either being rejected or having to reject others? One answer is to keep your search and screening preferences in mind at all times. Respond only to profiles in which you match the other person's preferences, and pursue relationships only with people who fit your criteria. Sounds simple, but sometimes people lose it online and do things that lead to hurt. Keeping your list of nonnegotiable traits uppermost in your mind will help keep your gut reactions in check so that you don't impulsively enter a relationship you will most likely break off anyway.

But no matter how careful you are in the screening process, you still will be faced with having to reject potential matches. If anyone told you that the anonymity and social distance of the Internet makes breaking up easier, he or she lied. Mercy and compassion are needed here more than in any other aspect of online dating.

In fact, you might be rejected by such a large number of people that you will wonder why you decided to subject your heart to this process. If you are a people pleaser who becomes paralyzed when you disappoint others, you will struggle. If your self-esteem is fragile and easily bruised, you will struggle as well. Many of the people who contact you will clearly not be who you are looking for, and you will have to shoot down their hopes. There is no way around being hurt and hurting others. Hurt may be rooted in disappointment, or it may come from someone who tramples on another person's feelings. There are rude and unmerciful people on the Internet, and you will have to stand out from these people and show the compassion and love of Christ even while you're disappointing someone (see Matthew 5:7).

When You Reject Someone

When you receive an e-mail or instant message from someone who is interested in you, but you don't share that person's interest, you have two choices. You can ignore the e-mail and hope the person gets the hint, or you can respond with a polite e-mail that sends a clear message that you're not interested. The vast majority of people choose the former, simply ignoring any additional e-mails from a person they're not interested in.

Jennifer, however, chose to send an explanatory e-mail to an unsuitable match.

"There was this one man who sent me an e-mail and his picture," she says. "I didn't find him anywhere close to attractive. His e-mail showed that he was too needy or desperate to find a wife. I struggled for days writing a reply. I'm sure this poor man has been rejected all his life, and here I was about to add to that. No matter what, I could never come out being the good guy. I sent him an e-mail trying to be positive but saying that I was talking to other men who were more compatible with me. I prayed that God would protect his heart and help him find the girl for him. I just wasn't that girl."

Jennifer rejected this man at stage 1 of her side of the relationship, but the man was already at stage 2, trying to establish first contact. Jennifer determined right away that he didn't possess enough of the nonnegotiable qualities she desired, so she gave him closure that was clear, yet compassionate. Sometimes, if you leave someone hanging by neglecting to respond to an initial e-mail, the person is left spinning his or her wheels, and that may hurt the person more than if you told him or her that you aren't interested.

Roger, a divorced store manager, knows about online rejection.

"Why don't women answer their e-mails?" he asks. "I know people are busy, but how hard is it to send some sort of reply? I would take a 'No, thanks. I'm not interested' over the black hole of silence any day. I sit there wondering if I said something wrong. I start wondering if maybe there's something wrong with me."

Those who feel like Roger need to depersonalize the lack of response to an e-mail. The people receiving the e-mail could be on vacation, away on business, or having computer trouble. The biggest mistake people make is to take a lack of response personally and lash out at the other person. Christians sometimes write e-mails or send instant messages that judge the other person. Even if the other person is treating you in an unloving way, you won't gain any points by lashing out. Just bless the person in your prayers or with an e-mail and move on.

If you decide to send an e-mail saying you're not interested, keep it short. There is no sense in prolonging the pain by rambling. Make sure you state *clearly* that you are not interested in pursuing a relationship, and don't confuse matters by saying, "We can still be friends." Using that line leads the other person to believe that he or she still has a chance. The person will then try to change your mind.

REJECTION LATER ON

The further your relationship progresses and develops, the more difficult rejection becomes. Don't disappear after you have engaged in online conversation with someone. April, a law student from Michigan, dated online for five months before finding the man who is now her husband.

"I met this incredible Christian man, and our first chat was four hours long," she says. "He kept saying how much we had in common and that God was up to something. The next day he sent me a virtual friendship card and thanked me for a wonderful chat. After several days we had moved to telephone conversations. I was so sure that he was the one. Then he just disappeared.

"At first I thought he was sick or hurt, and I kept calling and leaving messages. I sent him e-mails asking him to contact me. Then I found him in a chat room and sent him an instant message to see what was going on. He finally said he had changed his mind and didn't know how to break up with me. I told him how selfish his behavior was and how angry and hurt I was. He apologized and asked me for forgiveness.

"Once you get close to someone, you can't just disappear. It's not Christian. It's selfish and unloving."

April is right. You owe the other person closure, and that's even more important when the relationship has developed beyond stage 2. The method you use to break up should match the stage you were in at the time you decided you didn't want to continue the relationship. If you were e-mailing each other, then send an e-mail explaining the breakup. If you had moved to telephone contact, then make a phone call. And if you had moved your relationship offline, breaking up by e-mail or telephone is inappropriate. Treat the person's heart as you would want someone to treat your heart. If you reject someone with mercy and compassion, you will still cause disappointment and confusion, even hurt. But that is not the same as causing harm. Harm is when a Christian treats a person without compassion and self-sacrificing love. Simply disappearing causes harm, so don't do it.

AN IMPORTANT EXCEPTION: WHEN YOU *SHOULD* IGNORE SOMEONE

One of the most controversial aspects of online dating, especially for Christians, is deciding whether to respond to someone's initial e-mail, instant-message, or chat-room advances. There are plenty of times when it's best not to respond in the interest of your own safety.

But how can you determine whom you shouldn't respond to? Imagine you are stopped at a traffic light. Two people walk up and knock on your car window, trying to hit on you. Do you feel compelled to roll down your window and carry on a conversation? Or do you pray for the light to change so you can pull away? This analogy may sound preposterous, but it's not unlike what you encounter online. A multitude of strangers with varying levels of spiritual and emotional health will show up in your in-box, instant messages, message boards, and chat rooms. Some people are overtly strange or sinister, so it's easy to dismiss them without responding. The harder ones to read are the borderline people who are not outwardly strange or sinister but seem odd and possibly unhealthy.

People who are ungodly, unhealthy, abusive, or emotionally unstable try all sorts of schemes to force you into a relationship. Others, while not sinister, are emotionally or spiritually unhealthy, and they try to shame, guilt, or beg you to begin or remain in a relationship. If you can spot these types of people from their very first e-mail, their profile, or an instant message, you can shut off further involvement by ignoring the person. In these cases, complete silence is the best approach. Don't send an e-mail saying you're not interested because these people will read that as an opening to continue contacting you. You could very well set yourself up for cyberstalking.

Spotting Unhealthy People

There are ways to identify the people you should ignore. A person worth ignoring tends to

- send you sexually suggestive photos, e-mails, or instant messages;
- send you overly needy, desperate, or emotional e-mails or instant messages;
- send you angry or abusive e-mails or instant messages;
- send you odd e-mails or instant messages that ramble, fail to make a point, or lack a clear purpose;
- send you e-mails or instant messages professing undying love and commitment;
- send you e-mails or instant messages asking for financial assistance;
- divulge that he or she will commit suicide if you don't respond;

- heap guilt or shame on you for exercising cybersecurity; or
- send you e-mails or instant messages begging you to come back after you have clearly rejected or broken up with him or her.

Some people don't show their true character until after you have been e-mailing them for a while. In those cases, you need to abruptly break off all communication. If someone does anything online that makes you uncomfortable, you don't have to continue talking to that person. If someone tries to use guilt, shame, or anger to provoke you to continue communicating, you should run. (For a detailed discussion of cybersecurity, see chapter 9.)

WHEN YOU ARE BEING REJECTED

Being involved in online dating will expose you to rejection on a scale you have never faced before. Rejection comes in many forms, such as not receiving replies to your e-mails or instant messages, discovering that someone suddenly "disappears" after you have established a relationship, or receiving a "traditional" breakup notification. If a person suddenly disappears, don't beat yourself up, and don't let it damage your self-confidence. Also, be careful whom you turn to for support. Many Christians who don't understand or accept online relationships as being "real" won't be able to offer the support you need. Typically they will say, "Well, it's not like it was a *real* relationship." If you can't find offline support after a breakup, you might want to turn to an online Christian singles message board or other Christian singles online community.

If you find yourself being rejected repeatedly, you will need to determine whether you are doing something to contribute to your predicament. If you troubleshoot the situation and find that you didn't contribute to the rejection or breakup, then grieve the hurt and move on. Don't simply give up after being hurt a few times.

On the other hand, if you think you may have done something to cause the rejection, such as sending the wrong signals or sabotaging your success, then ask yourself the following questions about your most recent online rejection to see whether changes are in order:

- Did you read the other person's profile carefully to make sure that you have the qualities the person is looking for?
- Did you thoroughly fill out your profile and make sure that your descriptions are attractive, interesting, and memorable?
- Did you post a clear and attractive picture with your profile?
- Was your e-mail introduction positive, light, interesting, and memorable?
- Are you sure that you and your match were on the same page regarding the stage your relationship was at?
- Did you try to push too hard or too soon to move the relationship to the next stage?

Charles, a production assistant in Atlanta, had been divorced for almost a year and was unsure how to begin dating again. He was looking for someone who was the opposite of his ex-wife, who never seemed to appreciate his sensitive side.

When Charles began dating online, he described himself as a romantic poet in search of a woman who could appreciate a strong, sensitive Christian man. After two months, he met a few women but couldn't understand why he wasn't having success. Then he met Sarah, an online-dating veteran. Charles felt instantly drawn to her. Sarah was open, understanding, and witty.

After one long chat session, Charles told Sarah that he had met his soul mate. She told him she felt he was very nice, but she wanted him to slow down with the "soul mate" talk. Charles, however, began treating her like his girlfriend, using romantic nicknames, and talking as if she shared his level of interest. Sarah began pulling back and ignoring some of his many instant messages. Charles began pushing for an in-person date, but Sarah wanted out. After several days of being pressured by Charles for an in-person meeting, Sarah told him she had decided to pursue another match. Charles scrambled to tell her that he didn't want to lose her, and after a while, Sarah began ignoring his e-mails and disappeared.

I know both parties. Here is Sarah's side:

"I really liked Charles at first and thought things were promising. But after listening to him talk about his last relationship, I knew he was still hurt and was looking for someone just because he didn't want to be alone. All he could talk about was his ex-wife and how miserable he was. That kind of talk turned me off, and I would get silent. He kept saying I was his soul mate. All I did was listen to him so I could see if there was something there.

"I told him we were not on the same page, and then he got all needy and said that he couldn't lose me. He thought we were going to be together forever. I had to break it off much more harshly than I had ever done before."

Charles misinterpreted his early connection with Sarah as something unique and extraspecial. The Internet fosters quickly established, emotionally deep conversations unlike what you generally encounter offline during a similar stage of a relationship. In just a couple of days, you can know someone's hurts and fears. But Charles didn't understand that when you're online, deep conversations don't necessarily mean you have found your soul mate.

Charles was far too needy and selfish because of unresolved hurts. He thought Sarah shared his romantic feelings, so when she did not reciprocate, he panicked. The more he tried to hold on to the relationship, the more he pushed her away. Charles wanted to rush to exclusivity, and he forced a turning point with Sarah in which she chose to cease contact with him.

Factor God into the Equation

Sometimes you will receive very few quality responses to your profile because of something you included or failed to include. So go back and review your profile, your picture (if included), and your e-mail contacts for good style and appropriate substance. Have you been honest about portraying who you are in Christ? Have you displayed your heart, life, and dreams in a way that is attractive, interesting, and memorable? Have you sent positive and interesting e-mails to people? If so, then be still and remember that God is in control.

Because online dating puts you in a pool of hundreds of thousands of reasonably appropriate matches, it's easy to assume that you'll find your ideal partner and that it won't take that long. But don't fall into the trap of forgetting that God is sovereign, that He desires the best for you, and that your timing is not necessarily His timing.

Patience is a virtue, and with online dating it is essential. When you have done everything that is within your control, you need to let go and leave the process in God's hands. Trust Him to work—either by leading you to a deeper relationship with the other person or by allowing the relationship to die so you can move on toward other blessings He has in store for you.

Nine

Perverts, Players, Psychopaths, and Cyberstalkers

How to Stay Safe in Cyberspace

Would you give a stranger a key to your house? Would you go to a sexually oriented business or cruise bars until 4 a.m. just to meet other singles? Would you date a married person, hoping that he or she will get a divorce and marry you?

You may think I'm crazy for asking such questions, but these examples aren't much of an exaggeration when you consider what people do every day in cyberspace. Online daters often disregard the normal precautions they take in everyday life. It's as if they believe the Internet offers some invisible protection not available in the real world. It doesn't. Armed with information you have shared in your profile or e-mails, predators can do you real harm.

Taking appropriate precautions when you're online doesn't mean that you are paranoid, overly cynical, or living in fear. Jesus didn't endorse an unquestioning trust of others who have not earned your trust. As I moderate discussions in an online singles community, I often see singles advocate blind trust in anyone who claims to be a Christian. But when Jesus sent out His disciples, He issued a clear warning about the hidden motives of others: "I am sending you out like sheep among wolves. Therefore be as shrewd as snakes and as innocent as doves" (Matthew 10:16).

Caution involves wisdom and discernment, which Scripture commends. In daily life you may be surrounded by people who have impure motives, but you can observe clues, such as their behavior, and take adequate precautions. You also have people you trust who can give you input to help you protect yourself. But when you're online, the anonymity and global nature of cyberspace leaves you vulnerable. There are untold numbers of predators and wolves in sheep's clothing trying to gain your confidence so they can take advantage of your trust. When you date online, pray all the more for God's wisdom (see James 1:5-6).

INTERNET CAUTION

My intention in writing this chapter is not to scare you away from online dating but rather to make sure you are savvy when it comes to security so that you will know how to spot dangerous people online. Most of you will never meet people like this, but you still need to be aware of them and their online behavior.

It's important to realize that none of the risks discussed in this chapter are unique to the Internet. You could meet perverts, players, psychopaths, and stalkers offline as well. In everyday life we usually don't meet these kinds of people because we know where to go to ensure that those we are interacting with are safe. We tend to know the types of people we want to avoid and we know how to avoid them. We need to know these same things about the people we run across on the Internet.

Think of this chapter as a snapshot of people you want to avoid when you're online. And even though you may never meet an online pervert or predator, this information can serve as a valuable reference in case you ever have doubts about someone you meet on the Internet.

As you begin reading, remember that all types of dating carry some degree of risk. Being wise when dating on the Internet means being careful about how you present yourself, since even smart people can be taken advantage of. When you are savvy about online dating, the potential benefits can far outweigh the risks.

KNOW YOUR PREDATOR

Just because you haven't yet encountered (to your knowledge) a predator in cyberspace, it does not mean you won't stumble across one—or even attract one by something you say or do. Internet predators generally fall into three categories: perverts, players, and psychopaths. They victimize others for personal gain—whether it's for financial gain or to exert power over others, relieve boredom, or escape a bad living situation. You need to avoid these types of people at all costs.

Perverts

Pornography is the number one draw on the Internet, and pornographers target people who frequent all types of chat rooms and message boards. On unmoderated sites or those that disclose members' e-mail addresses, pornographers add the address lists to their own databases and begin sending out instant messages and e-mails. Owners of pornographic Web sites also purchase large numbers of Internet addresses so they can redirect people to their porn sites. You'll know this has happened when you end up at a porn site without intending to go there.

Once you are redirected to a porn site, if you don't have updated virus protection software or pop-up ad-blocker software installed, you might get stuck in a pornographic feedback loop. And you could easily contract a computer virus just from being on the site. Many of these viruses will set the home page for your Internet browser to a pornographic site. When you try to leave the site, scores of pop-up ads open with one sexually explicit image after another.

Sometimes pornographers contact you simply because you posted an ad on a singles Web site. They may send you an e-mail or instant message that says something like, "Hi, I saw your ad" or "Hi, do you want to chat?" When you open the e-mail, you could be exposed to a computer virus or sexually explicit material.

Perverts and other predators are not above posing as Christians. They pretend to be interested in an innocent relationship and frequently lurk in chat rooms, including Christian chat rooms. They initially approach you with inoffensive e-mails, and then after you begin dating, they become more sexually aggressive. Others are more straightforward but still might confuse you. If anyone sends you an e-mail or instant message asking, "Hi, do you want to cyber?" they are asking if you are interested in cybersex. They receive sexual gratification by talking dirty and describing sexual fantasies to strangers they meet online.

Robyn, a twenty-seven-year-old medical student from Houston, has been approached by Internet perverts. "If they send a sexualized picture, then of course you know what they are up to," she says. "But it may be hard to tell when they send you a picture that may or may not be sexual. Like why send me a picture of yourself without a shirt on? Sure, you are at the beach, but out of all the pictures you have, why send the one taken at the beach? The Bible says we should flee sexual immorality [see 1 Corinthians 6:18]. You better believe I'm fleeing with a pic like that.

"There is another type of man who tells you his sad story about being a slave to sexual sin back in the day, and he ends up talking about sex under the guise of sharing his past hurts. Talking about your past sex life to a perfect stranger is not romantic. It's gross. Or worse, some guys talk about their last girlfriend or ex-wife who had been sexually abused and

ended up not enjoying or wanting to have sex. Eventually the conversation will get around to your sexual preferences, history, and desires."

Even if you're not talking to a pervert online, chances are good that
you will eventually end up talking to someone who will want to discuss
sexual matters "in the interest of needing to know about sexual compatibility." The person may tell you that he just doesn't want to get burned
again like he did with his ex. The best course of action to take when this
happens is to just ignore the message.

Even some members of online Christian singles communities include
way too much personal information in their profiles. They may not be
predators, but they go into inappropriate detail about their sexuality.

So how can Christian singles maintain sexual purity in the midst of
all this detailed talk about sex? Since sex is an important component of
marriage, and since most online daters are hoping to eventually find a
spouse, at what point should you discuss issues of sexual compatibility? As
I mentioned in chapter 7, if certain aspects of sexual compatibility are
part of your nonnegotiable attributes for your ideal match, wait for an in-
person conversation that takes place only after you are talking seriously
about marriage. And have this conversation in the presence of a minister,
mentor, or Christian counselor. You will then be able to clarify any mis-
perceptions or misunderstandings. Having a reliable third party involved
will increase accountability and provide boundaries for the discussion, as
well as ease security concerns for women.

Players
Players are predators who play games with your mind and emotions. Players come in many forms:

Con artists. Beware of Internet Casanovas who profess undying love
to multiple people. They target singles who are extremely lonely as well as

those who are in love with the buzz they get from being in love. The victims hear what they want to hear and deny all the signs that the other person is a con artist.

Casanovas use your profile, e-mails, and chats to determine where you are most vulnerable. Then they tell you what you want to hear. Or you may find yourself in a close relationship with someone online, and it may seem perfectly understandable for this person to ask you for help. Your desire to help may get you in trouble. Internet Casanovas often shower a victim with gifts and attention so that the victim feels "special." Then, when the timing is right, the Casanova will bring up a crisis that gives the victim an opportunity to prove his or her love by doing something.

Watch for these clues:

- Casanovas often use overly romantic or poetic language and shower you with compliments.
- They send you gifts that are exactly what you wanted.
- They are smooth and always say the right thing.
- They often delay responding to you when you are chatting online. (Typically, a Casanova is juggling multiple chats at the same time.)
- After establishing a close relationship, he or she will give you a P.O. box number instead of a ground address or a home telephone number.

Online con artists often target Christians, telling us their sob stories because they know we are geared toward acts of service. These people describe their own chaotic, dramatic lives and want *you* to rescue them from their mess. Exercise extreme caution when someone starts using you as his or her therapist, social worker, or private banker. Sometimes the person with a sob story is not looking for money but is overly needy and becomes an emotional vampire who will suck the life out of you. Don't get involved. Allow the person to fix his or her own life.

Internet people. The term *Internet people* refers to a con involving invented, virtual people fabricated by someone who is bored but not necessarily mentally unstable. This con artist will use a unique screen name, find a picture of someone on the Internet, and then create a history and personality for an imaginary person.

Frank, a retired police officer who is divorced, fell victim to such a phantom. "I was clueless about the Net and met a person I thought was an attractive Christian girl. She was intelligent, funny, and interested in me. Then I received an e-mail from another girl who seemed even more perfect for me. She and I had more in common than the first one. I decided to focus on just one, so I broke up with the first girl. She said she was hurt and felt like I had led her on....

"After getting really close to the other woman, I asked about meeting her in person. I guess I should have noticed earlier that the two girls both made the same spelling mistakes and phrased things the same way. Then I got an instant message from the girl I was seeing, and she said she found out I was the man who dumped her best friend. I started comparing the e-mails and asked if they were from the same person. She, he, whoever just replied yes and then disappeared."

To help determine if you are dealing with an imaginary person, request more than one picture. Usually the people who are pretending to be someone else have only the one picture they snatched off someone else's profile. Also, moving to voice and video chats can help establish that someone is real. If the person refuses to send additional pictures or to participate in voice or video chats, then something is most likely not on the up and up.

Married but still looking. Married men and women sometimes keep their options open by dating online. Some are openly married and have close relationships with singles. Others pretend to be single, but in reality they are only separated and not legally divorced. These relationships might begin on nondating sites, such as general message boards or chat rooms and game sites. Two people strike up a conversation, and the married person begins to share struggles in his or her marriage. The single person wants to comfort the hurting married person. Over time the conversations and the sympathetic support that is offered develop into romantic feelings. The single person sides with the married person and often slips into an adulterous relationship online.

With such an intense extramarital relationship going on, there is little hope that the married couple will reconcile their marriage. Even if there is not any online or offline sex involved, such a relationship is a betrayal of the other person's marriage vows. Until someone is legally divorced, stay away from him or her.

Even if the person is divorced, you may want to learn more about the circumstances of the divorce before you pursue a relationship (see Matthew 19:9). If you decide to pursue a relationship with a divorced person without first having settled matters in your own mind and with God, you risk causing great harm by leading the person to believe you are okay with the divorce when in fact you are struggling to reconcile your convictions with your feelings for him or her.

Internationals seeking a partner. This scam involves international women pretending to fall in love with an unsuspecting man only to leave him once she receives American citizenship. Not everyone from overseas wants to scam you, but many do. One man who is willing to talk about his experience is Justin, a thirty-four-year-old computer programmer from Austin, Texas.

"I met the woman I wanted to marry online," says Justin. "She was from Russia, and I didn't care about the distance. When I went to Russia for the first time, I [felt that] she was everything I had dreamed of. When it was time for her to come to the States to visit my family, I paid for the trip because I didn't want to wait for her to save up enough money. When she got here, I was so in love with her I didn't think twice about giving her my credit card to treat herself nicely for the first time in her life. I trusted her.

"When I look at it now, it sounds like such a stupid thing to do. But we had been together for a year. She was going to be my wife. Why wouldn't I trust her? The day after we were married, my new bride went on a shopping spree that cost me more than a thousand dollars. Then she disappeared and told me in a note that things weren't going to work out.

"When I look back, I saw all the signs that she wasn't what she seemed to be, but I ignored them or explained them away. When the police learned that I met her online, they treated me like an idiot who deserved what he got."

Justin is now divorced from his Russian bride.

Experts in international dating highlight the following warning signs that indicate someone might be using you:

- The person asks you to move his or her family to your country once you are engaged or married.
- The person can't understand that just because you are considered wealthy by many developing-country standards does not mean you are wealthy by your own country's standards.
- The person, who is under thirty and extremely attractive, tries to convince you that he or she is ready to settle down.
- The person doesn't want you to meet his or her relatives who live in the United States.
- The person asks you to send money.

Minors pretending to be adults. Men especially need to pay close attention to this disturbing trend. Teenagers sometimes play games with unsuspecting adults by entering into online relationships. For example, let's say that during the course of online dating, an adult male develops feelings for a female teen whom he assumes is actually an adult. When the adult suggests an in-person meeting, the teenager might simply disappear. Or if the teen gets caught by her parents, to avoid punishment she might make up a story about being seduced online by the adult. The police are notified, and when the adult arrives for a dinner date with the person he met online, he is arrested. He may be able to prove that the minor lied to him, but it will take time and legal costs. In this instance, the adult will be assumed to be guilty.

If your online date disappears suddenly, the reason may be that he or she is a minor and got bored, caught, or preoccupied with other interests. Before you arrange for an offline meeting, make sure the person is a legal adult. Here are some ways to spot minors pretending to be adults online:

- They tend to have volatile emotions, get easily hurt, and need constant reassurance. Be alert for these and other signs of immaturity.
- They are frequently with someone else. When you are chatting online or on the phone, teens typically want to share the excitement with a friend. You may hear laughter or hushed talking in the background.
- They are hesitant to give specific information about their lives, such as when they graduated.

A woman who dates online posted this advice on a message board: "I had to find a way to protect myself from getting sucked into some fantasy [being played out by] a teenage boy. I came up with two questions. I first ask whom they voted for in the last election and why. Since there are some very intelligent kids out there, I knew I needed a second question. So I ask what they were doing when the *Challenger* blew up. I was seventeen when that happened. Everyone in my preferred age range would be able to tell me what they were doing when that tragedy happened."

The *Challenger* question is a good one for people who were at least in elementary school in January 1986. If you're seeking a match in a younger age group, you might want to come up with your own question.

Psychopaths and Cyberstalkers

Although most Christians who are dating online are normal, many in the online dating population are emotionally unhealthy. They have problems with relationships and display inappropriate emotions that are out of sync with the stage of relationship you are in.[1] If you meet someone online who displays the following behaviors, distance yourself from that person:

- Makes frantic attempts to keep you from leaving him or her or to convince you to reconsider a rejection or breakup.
- Swings back and forth between thinking you are perfect and claiming you are abusive or ungodly in your actions.
- Threatens suicide or displays impulsive and reckless behavior if you decide to leave the relationship or if you refuse to move to another level of relational intimacy.
- Exhibits frequent mood swings.
- Expresses chronic feelings of loneliness and emptiness.
- Displays sudden and frequent anger.
- Assumes your relationship is more intimate than it really is.
- Exaggerates his or her achievements and talents.
- Insists on being the center of attention.
- Expects you to automatically comply with his or her requests.
- Displays an unwillingness to apologize.
- Is unable to make decisions without first getting your advice and reassurance.

Serious psychopaths. A psychopath is more than just an odd or quirky person. A psychopath has an antisocial personality disorder and behaves in ways that are aggressive, amoral, criminal, or perverted. Psychopaths harm other people without remorse. If someone you meet online exhibits any of the following behaviors, flee:

- He or she does things that are grounds for arrest.
- He or she repeatedly lies or uses different aliases.
- He or she lacks anger-management skills.
- He or she lacks concern for the safety of self or others.
- He or she is unable to keep a job or pay bills.
- He or she shows little concern for having hurt another person.

If you encounter someone like this, take extreme care for your safety. Some of these traits may not show up until after you are in a relationship with the person. Women need to make sure they don't allow anyone to know where they live or work in case they need to break off the relationship. If you detect something that's just not right in the first contact e-mail, don't respond. Most people in this category are used to not receiving replies, so you aren't running the risk of standing out from the crowd. On the other hand, responding with a "not interested" might invite the person to stalk you online.

Make sure your profile doesn't include your location or your full name. Make sure your telephone number is unlisted. When you use your e-mail address, make sure it is not merely your name. And in all instances, keep your last name off the Internet. If you give too much information online for the entire world to see, you just may catch the eye of a predator.

Cyberstalkers. A cyberstalker is another type of online predator but is not necessarily a psychopath. Cyberstalkers use the Internet, e-mail, instant messaging, or other forms of electronic communication to harass or threaten people. Generally, in order for cyberstalking to be illegal, the cyberstalker has to threaten to harm another person. But if you are harassed online, check with the police in your area to find out the legal definition of stalking in your jurisdiction.

Many people find themselves being cyberstalked after they reject or break up with someone who came across as too jealous, demanding, or controlling. Cyberstalkers do not have to threaten you before their behavior is considered dangerous. Sometimes they will try to control you by threatening suicide if you don't do something they want, such as continuing the relationship.

Cyberstalkers use various techniques to track, harass, or threaten a person. One woman opened an e-mail attachment containing a virus that gave the stalker access to personal information on her computer. He stole her passwords and not only found out where she lived but also stole money from her bank account. So make sure your antivirus protection software is up-to-date, do not open e-mail attachments from questionable senders, and use firewall software protection on your computer, especially if you have a DSL or broadband connection.

Cyberstalkers can track AOL users through the buddy list. To minimize another person's ability to track your AOL activity, make sure you change your security preferences by limiting who can see you on their buddy list and send you instant messages or AOL greetings. People who know your e-mail address can put you on their buddy list without your permission. And even with the privacy settings, a person who knows your e-mail address can look you up in the AOL member directory to determine if you are online and where you are (e.g., in an AOL chat room or on an AOL message board).

So if you're an AOL user, keep your e-mail address private until you trust the other person one hundred percent. Open a free e-mail account with Yahoo! or Hotmail, or use Yahoo! for instant messaging. On Yahoo! you can chat with someone in instant messaging under the "invisible" mode so no one else will know you are online. Another advantage of Yahoo! is that people have to get permission before they can add you as a friend on their instant-messaging lists. If you use Yahoo! Web sites such as

Yahoo! Games, others can search your profile and tell that you are online if you do not specify in the privacy settings to keep your online status hidden. On Yahoo! however, once you have given a person permission to add you to his or her buddy list, you can't revoke that privilege. Therefore, if someone stalks you later, you will either have to change your Yahoo! ID or remain in invisible mode indefinitely.

If you are being cyberstalked, take immediate action. If your telephone number is listed, the person can find your address. If the stalker knows your full name, birth date, and the city you live in, he or she can search public records and find where you live. If you are being harassed online, make sure you keep all the e-mails, instant messages, your responses, chat transcripts, and other evidence, and ask the police in your area what you can do to protect yourself.

If you find yourself being cyberstalked, the following tips can help you cope:

- Tell the person harassing you in clear, firm language to stop harassing you and not to contact you again.
- Do not respond to any other messages the stalker sends you.
- If the problem persists, change your screen name or nicknames. You may also have to close your e-mail account and open a new one.
- If you are being harassed by e-mail, contact the harasser's ISP and register a complaint. Cyberstalking is against the Terms of Service policy for all ISPs, and they can close the person's account.
- If the person is a member of an online dating site, contact the manager of that site and alert him or her that you are experiencing harassment from one of his or her members.
- Stay out of chat rooms.

- Don't share your e-mail address or your chat or instant-messaging ID with anyone except trusted friends—and make sure you tell them not to share it with anyone.
- Make sure your online profiles do not include your age, sex, address, phone number, or where you work.
- Contact the police if a cyberstalker has threatened to harm you, if he or she knows where you live, or if you feel you or your family is in danger.

PROTECTING YOURSELF FROM PREDATORS

Here are three very practical ways you can protect yourself from all varieties of Internet predators:

1. Use an anonymous e-mail system. When you send e-mail, some identifying information about you and your ISP is right there in the headers of your e-mails. The numbers that appear in headers can be plugged into a publicly searchable database that will tell the person the name and location of your ISP. If you are using mail from large ISPs, such as AOL, Hotmail, or Yahoo! very little information is provided about your location. If, however, you have a regional ISP or access the Internet from work, plugging in the numbers of your e-mail header will indicate the region and possibly the city of your ISP.

To protect yourself when dating online, don't send e-mail from your work computer. You don't want stalkers showing up at your office. Also, make sure you remove your full name from your e-mail accounts so the "From" line in your e-mail reveals only your screen name or your first name. If a person has your full name and general location, he or she may be able to use a public-records database to find you.

AOL users should use a separate, free e-mail account when dating online and keep their AOL e-mail address private. Your AOL e-mail address is your screen name, and it would be too easy to cyberstalk you on AOL by using the Locate-Member feature.

Turn off your signature files or the option to send out your electronic business card. If you leave this feature engaged and choose instead to make a case-by-case determination of whether to send your signature or electronic business card, you may forget when you are busy shooting out e-mail responses and introductions to online inquiries.

Take advantage of the double-blind e-mail systems of online dating sites. Double-blind e-mail means that neither of you sees the other person's e-mail address unless that person chooses to disclose it. Some sites require members to log on to the group's site to send and read e-mails. Other sites forward e-mails to each person without letting either of you know the other person's e-mail address.

2. Get an unlisted telephone number. If you have a listed telephone number, someone can key in your name or your telephone number in an online search and find your home address. If you date online, pay the extra money for an unlisted telephone number. The quickest way to gauge your vulnerability to Internet predators is to go to online people-finder Web sites, such as *smartpages.com,* and search to see if you can be found. Also, check out the reverse phone number lookup feature. Enter your telephone number and see if your address appears. If you can find your own phone number online, then get an unlisted number.

Once your telephone carrier switches you to an unlisted number, contact the customer service department of the Web sites that have you listed and ask to be removed from their databases. Also, in an online dating relationship, if the relationship moves to telephone conversations, use a cell phone since cell numbers are not currently listed in telephone databases that reveal your address.

If you must use your home telephone, don't call a person collect from that phone. Your number will show up on the other person's telephone bill. Also, use the call block feature and refuse to call someone who has their anonymous call rejection (ACR) service engaged. And if you use the ACR service, you will need to deactivate it temporarily to accommodate a call from an online match who wishes to keep his or her number private.

3. *Know when it's time to bail.* The following warning signs were collected from people who have learned the hard way when dating online. It's a bright red flag if the person:

- requests money or anything else of value
- asks for or sends suggestive pictures
- makes excuses for not sending a picture
- provides inconsistent information about age, interests, upbringing, faith, job, and so on
- tells stories that don't make sense or are strange or implausible
- refuses to provide a home telephone number when you have reached an appropriate stage of the relationship
- forces you to ask permission before calling him or her
- is online at odd hours or only late at night
- reacts angrily if you call him or her unexpectedly
- is secretive
- pressures you to move to another stage in the relationship
- looks nothing like his or her picture or behaves in a vastly different way from how he or she comes across online
- won't introduce you to family and friends
- resists moving to offline status, despite expressing the desire to marry
- seems to have a different living arrangement than what he or she told you about (e.g., a baby is crying, a dog is barking, a commuter train rattles by when you are talking on the phone)
- is flirtatious or too flattering

- asks you how much money you earn or asks other questions that would provide a clue to your net worth
- seems too perfect, too successful, and/or too holy
- asks you too many questions while not giving out much personal information
- brags about having a high-status, well-paying job
- if the person is male, demands submission and questions a woman's Christianity if she does not comply with his requests
- doesn't listen to you or doesn't remember what you say
- is hurt, offended, or questions your love when you exercise cybersecurity
- is caught in lies, exaggerations, and half-truths

Put on Your Armor

This might have been a scary chapter to read, but none of this information was intended to scare you away from online dating. Most people who date online never meet any of the predators described here. But as you practice appropriate cybersecurity, don't forget to also seek God's protection. Keep yourself clothed in the full armor of God while you are online so you can resist the schemes of the Enemy (see Ephesians 6:10-18). And always pray for wisdom and discernment (see James 1:5).

Making wise choices online will save you many headaches and much heartache. Stepping outside of God's will or choosing to go off on your own without input from trusted friends or mentors will only increase the likelihood of meeting a pervert, a player, a psychopath, or a stalker online.

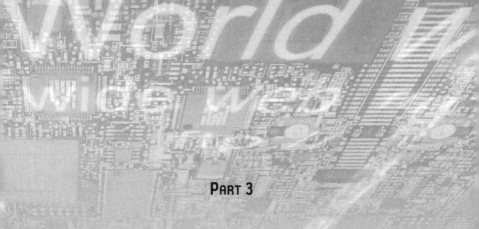

PART 3

You Met Someone Special— Now What?

Love is patient, love is kind. It does
not envy, it does not boast, it is not proud.
It is not rude, it is not self-seeking, it is
not easily angered, it keeps no record of
wrongs. Love does not delight in evil
but rejoices with the truth. It always
protects, always trusts, always hopes,
always perseveres. Love never fails.

—1 CORINTHIANS 13:4-8

Ten

Is He (or She) "the One"?

How to Narrow the Field and Recognize Your Best Match

O nce you have made first contact with someone you meet online, you'll discover that online dating demands a significant time commitment to mature the relationship. Why so much time? Because it takes awhile to get enough information to make decisions on whether to stay or to leave a relationship in search of a better match.

As you date online, you may notice many profiles that come close to fitting your ideal match. And you will receive e-mail from others who see you as a potential match. Most online daters manage several contacts simultaneously instead of talking exclusively to one person until they have enough information to make a decision. If you've met several people you are attracted to online, you might be wondering what to do next. Or if you and an online date both feel a strong mutual attraction, you might wonder when it's time to take your profile down and focus on just one person.

As you manage your contacts with various online dates, you may have to disable your profile for a while just so you'll have enough time to focus on the contacts you already have. This doesn't mean you're committing to any of the current matches; it just means that you're protecting your time and attention so you can make the best decision.

"I thought I was in over my head the day I was juggling five chats at the same time," says Allison, a twenty-four-year-old writer who has been dating online for a year. "I couldn't focus on any of them and thought I wasn't accomplishing anything.

"Being attracted to more than one person is not easy because you have to split yourself to talk to everyone just to get to know each of them better. I e-mail and chat with a man long enough to see if there is something worth pursuing, and then I force myself to make a decision. Otherwise the computer will eat up all my time."

Managing online relationships that are at differing stages can be confusing. This is a good time to pull out your Essential Qualities Matrix from chapter 5. Use it to help yourself focus conversations on topics that will reveal whether a date possesses attributes that you have on your list. If all the matches seem wonderful and you don't know how to make a decision, create a compare-and-contrast chart to visually represent your relationships and how each person stacks up. The following Match Comparison Matrix can help you sort through your matches.

The Match Comparison Matrix

Prepare a chart similar to the chart on page 174 to see at a glance how close various matches are to your ideal match. First, list all of the attributes you consider essential in an ideal match. (Included in the sample matrix are some of the common essential attributes people use.) Then list the desirable but optional traits. Across the top of the matrix, fill in the names of your online dates, and then mark the applicable attributes for each match to see how closely each one fits your predetermined criteria.

Trina, the online dater mentioned in chapter 7, first used the Essential Qualities Matrix to evaluate incoming matches and determine which ones were close enough to her ideal match to warrant pursuing the relationship further. Then she used the Match Comparison Matrix to compare matches side by side when she had more than one suitable match to consider. Eventually, she could do the comparison in her mind rather than pulling out pen and paper.

It's simple to use the Match Comparison Matrix. You already know the essential and optional attributes you are looking for in your ideal match. By keeping those attributes in the front of your mind, you can plug in the names of your matches and see how closely each one comes to meeting your ideal criteria. It will become clear as well how the matches compare with one another.

After you complete the checklist, notice which attributes differ among your matches and determine which matches fail to possess traits that you have determined are essential. Afterward, ask yourself these questions:

- Which match, if any, has *more* of the essential qualities from the matrix?
- Which match, if any, has *more* of the combined qualities I'm looking for (both essential and optional)?
- Between the matches being compared, which one has the greatest number of qualities that are most important to me?
- Does this person possess a fatal flaw—a quality that's a deal breaker, such as children from a previous marriage, heavy debt, or different religious views?
- Since no candidate will be a perfect match, is the leading match a person who possesses some nonessential characteristics that make up for not possessing all of the essential traits?

If you start making exceptions to your list of essential traits, ask yourself if you're making the change(s) to force your criteria fit a person rather than waiting to find a person who better fits your essential criteria.

"I went online and within a week I narrowed the field to three men," says Christine, a graduate student. "I prayed about it, looked at them side by side, and learned that I needed to know more. I had just one fatal flaw listed, and that was how a person felt about children. I wanted more than one.

Match Comparison Matrix				
Attribute	*Ideal Match*	*Match 1*	*Match 2*	*Match 3*
ESSENTIAL ATTRIBUTES				
Age				
Church Affiliation				
Marital History				
Children at Home				
Occupation				
Ministry Involvement				
OPTIONAL ATTRIBUTES				

"I was able to whittle down my list using that criterion. I had two left and just kept talking to both of them and writing down their responses in my journal. I needed to make sure I could remember it all. After a while, I discovered that I had another deal breaker. I wanted to continue working, and although I didn't mind working from home while my children were little, I didn't want to give up my career. One of the two men had definite ideas about a woman's role in the household. So I was able to whittle things down to just Ray, and we've been dating for almost a year."

Some people resist the systematic process of evaluating matches, arguing that in real life people make decisions based on feelings, not a checklist. In response I say simply that online dating is not like offline dating. If you make a decision based only on passion or the heat of the moment, you could miss a fatal flaw that you would notice fairly easily by using a checklist. Also, when you date online, you interact with far too many people to even contemplate getting emotionally involved with all of them. It's smart to develop a process for sorting, evaluating, and deciding which matches are most compatible. After a short period, you will internalize your ideal match list, so you won't always be pulling out a checklist to fill out.

SLOW DOWN!

In chapter 7 we looked at the stages of an online relationship. As you correspond with matches, make sure you both are on the same page as to what stage the relationship is in.

"Jacki and I had been talking for a while," says Corey, an artist from Dallas, "but I wasn't sure she was the one. So I left my profile up and kept screening e-mails. When I saw someone interesting, I looked at the profile just in case. I didn't feel like I was cheating because Jacki and I weren't exclusive, and I made sure I didn't lead her into thinking that we were anything other than friends. But she saw that I had been active in my profile, and she was hurt."

After Jacki and Corey had been talking for a few months, she took down her profile, which signaled she was serious about the relationship leading to marriage. She was at exclusive status, while Corey was still in search mode. Needless to say, their relationship fizzled.

One of the most confusing questions related to online dating is, When is a couple really "dating"? And if they agree they are dating, when are they exclusive? To minimize confusion when you are still in search mode, try the following:

- Don't use poetic or romantic talk.
- Don't talk about your future together.
- Don't use the term *soul mate*.
- If you sense the other person is falling for you and you're not there yet, talk about it.
- Never make it seem as if there is something special or unique about your conversations or relationship until you are ready to become exclusive.

When you are still in search mode, consider the impact your words have on the other person. You are nothing more than friends until you both agree to become exclusive. So prior to that point, refrain from romantic talk. If you speak in romantic terms while continuing to date others, you're being dishonest. Romance is not meant to be spread around, so keep things on a friendship level for now.

Until you both agree that your relationship is exclusive, there is no need for either of you to take down your profile. Don't pressure the other person to decide on the exclusivity of the relationship until he or she is ready. Pressure will drive him or her away.

As you take things slowly, you may eventually get serious about the other person. That's the time to bring up the subject of taking down profiles. Don't play the game of taking down your profile and waiting to see if the other person will do likewise. Just be open about your feelings and talk together about the issue.

Before you reach this point, though, develop some signposts that will indicate that it's time to take down your profile. Doing this in advance will help you make a more rational decision. The following signposts have worked for other couples:

- You have been communicating with one particular match for _____ weeks/months.
- You have prayed about the decision and know that the timing is right to explore a relationship with just one match.
- You are confident that if you take down your profile, you won't wonder if you are missing out on a better person.
- You and your match have discussed your feelings toward each other and have agreed to be exclusive partners and to take down your profiles.

ARE YOU HEADED FOR HEARTBREAK?

Dating online, like dating offline, often yields some promising results that may lead only to a dead end. Rather than letting dead ends deepen your sense of rejection, consider them as learning experiences. You can take something away from each failed match that will help you in future relationships.

Many online daters have been hurt by relationships that start fast, heat up quickly, and then suddenly burn out. Sometimes the other person simply disappears. There is no sense of closure. Sometimes individuals disappear because they have been dishonest and don't care to continue the deception. In those cases, you aren't guilty of driving them away, and it's best the relationship ended. There are other instances, however, where you may fail to recognize that you are in a fantasy or one-sided relationship that is destined to end. In those instances, you may be inviting heartbreak.

A fantasy relationship is romanticized and idealized—the perfect relationship you've been longing for. These relationships are fueled by the strong feelings of one person but are not reciprocated by the other person. Heartbreak is guaranteed because the two people are out of step with each other. The person who is in love with being in love actually hastens a breakup by refusing to let go of the fantasy in hopes that the other person will come around.

If you are convinced you have found "the one," evaluate your relationship—and see if you're at risk—by indicating whether you agree or disagree with the following statements. Don't invite heartbreak.

Heartbreak Predictor

1. Your relationship had instant intimacy, and it is taking very little effort to keep it at that level of intensity.

   Agree   Disagree

2. You go to great lengths to avoid arguments or conflict in an effort to keep the relationship perfect.

   Agree   Disagree

3. You are the only one making sacrifices of time or expense to keep the relationship close.

   Agree   Disagree

4. You spend time thinking of all the ways you can take care of the other person.

   Agree   Disagree

5. You are the only one who talks about the romantic things you and your match will do when you meet in person.

Agree   Disagree

6. Your relationship is perfect; the two of you have never had a disagreement.

Agree   Disagree

7. The other person fits your ideal match one hundred percent.

Agree   Disagree

8. You talk about your love and your future together more than your match does.

Agree   Disagree

9. You explain away any problems that come up.

Agree   Disagree

10. You believe your relationship is everything you hoped for, but your match has yet to say the same thing.

Agree   Disagree

11. Your match appears to have no annoying habits or quirks.

Agree   Disagree

12. Your conversations are like the movies, full of poetry and romance.

Agree   Disagree

13. You withhold sharing unpleasant or negative feelings to keep the other person happy and the relationship peaceful.

Agree   Disagree

14. You hide any habits that might annoy your match.

Agree   Disagree

15. You feel that with your match at your side, you will never be lonely again.

Agree   Disagree

16. Since meeting your match, you suddenly have fewer problems.

    Agree   Disagree

17. Although your match doesn't have many of the qualities on your list, your intuition still tells you the relationship is perfect.

    Agree   Disagree

18. You harbor some feelings of hurt or resentment deep down because of some of your match's behavior (such as forgetting to call, failing to be on time for a chat, etc.), but you are afraid to say anything.

    Agree   Disagree

19. Your relationship is always exciting.

    Agree   Disagree

If you agreed with more than five of the nineteen statements, slow down before your heart gets broken. We all know that when the high of love hits us, we don't recognize bad or annoying traits in the other person. It's like that at first, but if you think you're getting serious with someone, you need to wake up and make sure you're not heading for heartbreak. Look at your relationship realistically. Check for any warning signs that the two of you may not be on the same page.

FALLING FOR MORE THAN ONE PERSON

In online dating it's possible to fall for more than one person at the same time. If you have strong feelings for two people, it will be hard to choose between them. And each of the other people may feel the same way toward you as well. Can you imagine the heartbreak that will happen when you have to choose just one?

Savvy online daters stop themselves before they get close to more than one person at a time. Whenever they feel strongly that a serious and long-term relationship can occur, or they begin to feel as if they are falling for a person, they choose one match and end conversations with other people.

"I met three wonderful Christian women online, but I met them at different points," says Chad, a divorced man in his thirties. "Alexa wasn't too easy to talk to at first, so it took longer to get to know her. Then I met Karen, and I still hadn't learned too much about Alexa. Then Lindsey came along, and she and I clicked instantly. All three fit what I was looking for.

"I could tell that Alexa was falling for me, and I didn't want to be rushed into choosing her just because she fell for me first. What if I chose wrong and messed up everything? It's not like I could go back to the other ones."

Chad did choose Alexa, but he had to have two very painful breakup conversations with the other women. He caused more hurt because he didn't know how to make a choice at the right time.

WHEN ONLINE CHEMISTRY DOESN'T SURVIVE OFFLINE

A cardinal rule of online dating is to wait until *after* you have met someone in person before you conclude that you have found your ideal match. Trina is one of my good friends. After she met Robert on a Christian matchmaker site, she called me screaming for joy that she had met her soul mate: "Cheryl, he said that my profile read like the Proverbs 31 wife he has been seeking!"

Here we go again with the Proverbs 31 thing. I was glad we were talking over the phone because I rolled my eyes. But I kept my mouth closed.

"He writes these amazing e-mails that just penetrate your soul. I can feel how much he is in love with the Lord. I know you think I'm crazy, but I can just feel it. Robert is 'the one.'"

I was concerned that my cautious and spiritually mature friend was moving so quickly. She talked for hours about how much she and Robert had in common. When they exchanged pictures, they were still engrossed. I wanted to make sure that before she considered Robert to be her soul mate, she knew all about his faith. And since they were expressing deep feelings for each other, they definitely needed to meet offline in the near future.

It took almost a year for Robert to save enough money to visit Trina. I accompanied her to the airport to pick him up, and I saw the almost-instant disappointment on both their faces. Trina was heavier and taller than Robert had imagined, while Robert was much older and had "awful teeth," according to Trina. They felt no physical attraction. Actually, Trina would feel a bit sick every time Robert smiled.

Strike one!

While they waited in baggage claim, I started to squirm at how painfully slow and disjointed their conversation was. I could understand a little nervousness, but this went far beyond nerves. Trina had described Robert as a witty, extroverted man who had a commanding knowledge of the Bible. In real life, though, it became clear that Robert was an extreme introvert. Each sentence was an exercise in excruciatingly deliberate word choice. Trina, meanwhile, is a public-relations consultant, so her life is in the spotlight and she draws her energy from being around people.

When Robert told her that he didn't like large gatherings, Trina modified her plans so they could attend a Bible study with just eight people. At that gathering, it was clear that Robert did have a strong knowledge of the Bible, but he stood in the corner and made only four comments the entire night.

Trina whispered to me, "Cheryl, he sucks the life out of the room."

The discrepancy between the online Robert and the offline Robert was staggering.

Strike two!

During Robert and Trina's in-person meeting, they had to adjust their online fantasy images to fit clear-eyed reality. They were too spiritually mature to let physical appearance alone be the deal breaker. But face to face they were learning about the power of nonverbal communication in feeding or deflating chemistry. They connected powerfully through the written word, but as much as 90 percent of information is conveyed through nonverbal communication. For example, Trina wore more makeup than Robert preferred. And in Trina's opinion, Robert's social skills were stunted. The chemistry just wasn't there.

Strike three!

Trina and Robert had a long talk and spent the rest of the weekend as friends. Because they had built a solid relationship in Christ online, they have maintained their friendship for more than four years—and both are now married to other people. They learned that impressions made through online communication can never be taken as the final word. Your feelings must be confirmed through an in-person meeting. And for many, a soul-mate connection does not become evident until after years of friendship. It can be a gradual thing; it doesn't have to be instant to be valid.

HANDLING SENSITIVE SUBJECTS

So you think you have met "the one." Have you held back on disclosing anything because you were waiting for just the right moment? Well, now is the time to fess up. There is a real possibility that the other person may not accept whatever you've been concealing. He or she may walk away from the relationship. There is very little you can do in this situation, so leave it in God's hands.

If you have sensitive information to reveal, make sure you pick a time and a mode of communication that are well suited for the seriousness of what you are disclosing. Some topics are best left out of e-mail and other written communication. Some topics can be discussed by chat or telephone, but others should be discussed only in person. The following subjects are best raised later in your relationship and should be discussed in video chat or in person:

- past experience with abuse or trauma
- criminal background
- a history of wild living (your before-Christ days or prodigal years as a Christian)
- details of a divorce and your current relationship with your ex
- problems with your children or your desire for more children
- weight or body issues or discussions about body art and piercings
- financial health (e.g., bankruptcy, heavy debt, credit problems, unemployment, child support)
- a disability, chronic illness, or disfigurement (those hidden under clothes or makeup)

How do you decide when to discuss such issues, and how do you decide the best way to have the discussion? Pray about the timing and look for an opportunity after you know the strength of the other person's character and faith. Then you'll be more certain that your news will fall on compassionate and accepting ears. At least you hope for this outcome. Sometimes the other person may choose to end the relationship after your disclosure. I was born with a physical disability and know from personal experience how difficult it is to discuss my disability in dating situations. But don't allow your normal fears to keep you from disclosing sensitive information.

EXPLORE YOUR OWN FEELINGS

Singles with sensitive issues to disclose need to deal with their own feelings before trying to discuss an issue with their match. Some of the most common feelings to explore are:

- fear that you'll be rejected because of your problem
- anger about the unfairness of being rejected or judged in the past
- feelings of shame about the problem or about your role in causing it
- feelings of despair because you think you'll never be loved
- frustration because you are tired of this one thing holding your life back

Don't feel shame or guilt over having any of these feelings. God knows your hurts and fears. But so does Satan, and he wants you to believe that all of your problems, especially those in your love life, are caused by whatever sensitive issue you have in your past. Sometimes your unresolved feelings can force you to react in ways that can ruin a relationship.

To help guard against subverting a relationship, check your past behavior to see if you have unknowingly sabotaged the relationship before you gave the other person a chance to hear you out and accept you for who you are.

- Did you bail out before you disclosed sensitive details because you expected to be rejected?
- Did you start nitpicking or being hard to please in order to push the person away?
- Did you disclose personal details using a defensive tone while expecting instant, 100 percent acceptance as proof of the person's genuine love?
- Did you hold off disclosing details in hopes the relationship would reach the emotional point of no return in which the person would be so in love with you that your disclosure wouldn't matter?

Again, timing and forthrightness are the key factors. If you try to hold off disclosing sensitive matters until you are appropriately close to the person, you may never feel close enough to bring up the topic. Or you might wait too long, causing the person who is now attached to you to wonder if you've been hiding other things. Also, remaining silent for too long can cause you to hold back emotionally, which can also harm the relationship. On the other hand, if you discuss an issue too soon, you may overwhelm the person before he or she has a strong enough emotional attachment to you.

Kevin knows the difficulty of timing when it comes to disclosing a sensitive personal issue. He has a chronic illness, Crohn's disease, which he needed to discuss with an online match.

"I look normal," he says, "but I didn't date much because it seemed like no one could handle my situation. I had my colon removed, and I have to use a bag [to collect the waste].

"I went online just to talk with other Christian singles. I was not interested in dating because I didn't feel like being rejected all the time. I met Regina, and we were just friends. After a while, our friendship developed into more.

"While we were friends, I worried about telling her about my disease. But she had some physical problems too. She told me I couldn't control other people. All I could do is pray about how to talk about my disease and then talk about it without being negative or defensive. After that, it's the other person's choice to stay or leave, and that choice has nothing to do with me. The day she told me this, I knew I wanted to marry her. She really understood me down to my heart."

Regina and Kevin are now married. Her insight should relieve some of the pressure you might feel if you're struggling over when and how to disclose sensitive personal details. It's hard to keep your self-esteem out of it, but the other person's reaction or decision does not mean that you are a second-class person or that you will never find someone who will accept you. Remember the following guidelines:

- You can't control the reaction or decisions of the other person.
- Pray about the right time to disclose your information, and ask God to protect your heart.
- Disclose your information in a nondefensive way so that the other person won't be reacting to the chip on your shoulder.
- Discuss the issue in person if at all possible. The more complicated the issue, the more you will need to clarify yourself. So talk in real time.
- Allow time for your news to settle in and for the other person to process everything. Depending on the magnitude of what you disclose, it might take longer for him or her to take it in. Give the person a few days to think and pray about his or her feelings.
- Accept whatever happens. Don't try to shame or guilt the person if he or she chooses to leave. Calmly express disappointment, and then mourn and move on. It's his or her choice and does not reflect on your worth or beauty.

I've been in this situation many times. I have had several spine fusions, so I have to use crutches or a scooter to get around. There are many physical activities I can't get involved in, but that doesn't mean I face nothing but limitations. I may not be able to run a marathon, go skiing, or hike in the mountains, but my limitations don't prevent me from doing most of the things everyone else enjoys. I love to travel. In fact, I climbed the stairs of the Great Wall of China. When people meet me offline, it's pretty hard not to see me as a person first.

Online, I have chosen not to post a picture of myself using crutches or in my wheelchair because I don't want people to see a condition before they see the person I really am. I don't want others to focus on the few things I can't do. Therefore, I choose for others to get to know me first as a person. Later I disclose my disability.

Regardless of my vibrant life and contentment with who God created me to be, some Christians have chosen to walk away from a dating relationship with me. Many people, including Christians, just don't picture themselves dating or marrying a person who has a disability. Some Christians have told me that they don't want to give up on their dreams of doing rugged, outdoors-oriented things with their spouse. Some confess that they're not strong enough to deal with the hassles of having to negotiate an inaccessible world.

I typically leave the situation on a positive note because I learned a long time ago that it's not me, it's them. When you grow up with a disability and face ridicule and rejection, you end up either bitter or with a tough spirit that refuses to internalize the negative attitudes of others.

It's All in God's Hands

Some of the most painful mistakes happen when a couple reaches the exclusive stage in the online dating process. The "instant" intimacy that the Internet breeds can fuel impatience, which can lead to poor decisions. Far too many Christians get online, nurse a relationship to an exclusive status, and then panic that the person they believe is "the one" might back out. This type of fear does not come from God. And if left unchecked, it will more than likely destroy the relationship.

Your life is in God's hands, so remain in prayer from the very beginning of your online journey. When you find the person you think is "the one," make sure you slow down and put the relationship in God's hands.

Remain patient and let God lead you. You won't regret it.

Eleven

From Virtual to Reality

Setting Up Your First In-Person Date

Research indicates that most matches made online never make it to an in-person meeting because most couples decide to bail out long before the relationship reaches this stage. For those who plan to meet in person, distance, schedules, and the expense of travel make it a challenge. So if you and your match are moving toward an in-person date, you've reached an important milestone.

If you're in an exclusive online relationship, you'll know it's time to meet face to face when any of the following occur:

- You feel a strong attachment and deep connection with the other person.
- You feel as if you're falling in love.
- You are willing to consider moving to another city to live closer to your match. (Yes, many people have these feelings before actually meeting in person.)
- You have begun to plan your wedding—if only in your imagination.

PREPARE FOR THE BEST FIRST DATE

In your first offline date, you want to confirm the chemistry you have developed online. Even when both of you have been open and completely honest in e-mail and telephone conversations, it's still possible to develop a faulty picture of what the other person is really like. You need to confirm your impressions and hunches through an in-person date.

If you're starting to make arrangements for a face-to-face date, now is the time to give your match a heads-up on any sensitive subjects (see chapter 10). Your issue doesn't have to be a biggie like a chronic illness or disfiguring injury. It could simply be that you're uncomfortable in crowds, have trouble hearing in noisy restaurants, or have certain allergies or special dietary requirements. Discuss these now to avoid any unsettling surprises later.

Now is also the time to come clean if you haven't always been upfront about the things you've discussed online and by telephone. Clarify any discrepancies regarding your age, hair color, height, weight, and other details of your physical appearance. If the two of you have not exchanged pictures, make sure you do before you invest time and money in traveling. No one wants to greet a date only to suffer the pain of seeing disappointment on the other person's face.

Justin was living in Australia when he met Nicole, a Chicagoan, online. They dated for a year before meeting in person. It took that long for Justin to save up for a trip to the United States.

"We were married just one week after we met in person," Nicole says. "I knew we had been honest with each other the whole time. I heard all the horror stories about dating on the Net, but for the most part, if you have two honest Christians [dating online], I think they will find little to be surprised at when they meet. When I met Justin, he was exactly like I imagined."

"We exchanged tons of pictures during that year [of dating online]," Justin says. "Every time I went somewhere or did something, I'd take a picture and e-mail it to Nicole so she could see what a typical day in my life was like. She did the same thing. Nicole bought a Web cam and convinced me to get one, and we had video chats all the time. So when we met we weren't surprised in a bad way. I was struck at how much more beautiful she was in real life."

Couples who date online tend to share more information—going deeper more quickly—than couples who begin a relationship by meeting in person. Those who take advantage of the benefits of Internet dating can build solid relationships that continue growing when they move their relationship offline. The key is being completely honest from the beginning.

Another factor that will help assure the success of a first in-person meeting is for both parties to be grounded in reality. Recognize that even the most forthright person you date online will not be exactly whom you expected. How many times have you met a client or business associate whom you've talked to for months by e-mail and telephone? Usually the person looks nothing like what you had pictured. This tendency shifts into overdrive when you are dating online. Your imagination fills in any information gaps with data pulled from your idea of the ideal mate. Even after you exchange pictures, your brain will continue to fill in the void about how the two of you will interact when you meet offline. When you finally do meet in person, your mental images may or may not be a close approximation of the person standing in front of you.

In-Person Guidelines

You should already know each other well before you start arranging your first in-person date, but you still won't know *everything* about the other person. Because you haven't met before in person, it's wise to come up with a contingency plan. This will give you a ready-made excuse if the first date goes badly, and it will protect you if your online match turns out to be completely different in person. Don't make the mistake of thinking your match is so wonderful that nothing could possibly go wrong when you meet for the first time.

Veterans of online dating offer the following guidelines for your first in-person date:

1. Try a double date or a group date. For your first offline date, consider bringing another couple along or meeting a small group of friends for coffee. This is wise not just from a safety standpoint. It's also helpful to have others around to add to the conversation.

Having a few friends or another couple present relieves a lot of pressure. Both you and your date will be nervous, and you'll both want to make the very best impression. But it's hard to feel at ease when it's just the two of you. Adding a few other people to the mix will allow you to avoid painful gaps in conversation. Also, having a friend along can provide a needed distraction in case you or your date is disappointed or surprised when you meet in person.

Here's an added benefit: If you take a friend along, you can ask the friend later what he or she thought about your date. Getting that third-person perspective right after the first date might be the best thing you can do.

2. Meet in public. Plan to meet your date in a public place. It's best to have other people around, even if they're strangers. If you fly to another city to meet your match, make sure you rent your own car and arrange for your own lodging. Also, don't feel that you have to meet each other at the airport. It sounds romantic, I know, but give the other person time to freshen up from the trip before you meet.

Plan a low-pressure activity that will allow for relaxed conversation. Even if you love hiking or going for long walks on the beach, avoid going to a secluded spot on your first date. Choose a coffee shop or a casual restaurant. Drive separately and plan to meet inside. For now, don't ask your date to pick you up at home or at work. I know, I know. It's romantic to have a man pick you up and open your door. But all of that can come later.

Also, make sure to choose a meeting place where you can talk. Don't go straight to a movie, for instance, where you'll be spending two hours together in silence. If you both love movies and just have to see the latest romantic comedy, then have dinner beforehand so you'll have a chance to get past the awkward small-talk phase.

3. Keep your date short. While you are hoping for blissful hours spent together, don't plan more than a couple of blissful hours on your first date. Long, lingering dates can come later. Plan in advance to keep your first date short. If you don't and instead organize a full afternoon or evening of activities, then you won't have an easy way to cut the date short if things start heading south.

Of course, you'll probably hit it off when you meet. In that case you can always revise the original plan and tack on a second short activity. You can meet initially for coffee, and if that goes well, then you might suggest continuing the conversation across the street at a favorite pizza joint. But make sure that the advance plan, understood by both of you, is for something simple and short. That way you'll have a ready-made out if things don't go smoothly and you need time to think or to get feedback from a friend.

Keep it short even if things go really, really well. Give yourself time to cool down and reflect. Talk things over with a friend. Get some perspective before going on your second date.

4. Stay close to home. Don't take your date to a place you've never been before. You want to know in advance that the food is good and the setting is quiet enough for you to carry on a conversation. Also, you want to be in a part of town where you know the streets, the homes of acquaintances, and the places where there will be crowds. Remaining in familiar areas increases the safety factor, and knowing the setting will be conducive to getting to know each other.

If you are the one traveling to meet your date, you can maintain a level of control and security by driving yourself and arranging your own lodging. It's a good idea to keep the hotel, and especially your room number, secret. If your date needs to call, he or she can call your cell phone. If you don't have a cell phone, I'd strongly encourage you to buy, rent, or borrow one before you meet your date in person. Everyone needs a safety zone in case the date goes badly.

5. Keep a friend informed. Whether you are traveling to meet your match or hosting your date, leave the person's profile and your itinerary with a friend or family member. Make sure someone can find you in case you don't return when expected. A delay might be nothing more than losing track of time, but it's good to know that someone knows where you're supposed to be. And there is always the possibility that something could go wrong with the date. You might ask a friend to call your cell phone at a certain time in case you need an excuse to cut the date short. If you can't arrange for a friend to call you, you can always call an elderly relative or a neighbor whom you know is usually home. That way your date will feel that someone other than the two of you know where you are.

6. Be vigilant. Never leave your purse, your backpack, or your wallet unattended. Likewise, if you leave the table during a meal, order a fresh drink when you return. You probably think I'm bordering on paranoia here. But until you know him or her better, take care of yourself. Unattended drinks are vulnerable to people who may use a date-rape drug.

7. Stay cool and take it slowly. Although you already know a lot about your online match, treat your first in-person date as if you're meeting for the first time. Keep the candlelit dinners, hugs, kissing, and other "couple" behaviors out of the mix for now. This is a confirmation date, not a proposal of marriage. You are confirming whether you want this relationship to continue for a second date.

Many women complain that following precautions such as these makes them feel rude or inconsiderate. If you feel that way, remember that a man who has your well-being at heart will want you to feel safe and secure. It's a huge red flag if you are taking ordinary precautions and the other person asks, "Don't you trust me?" or "I thought you loved me." A person who is acting in love will not pressure you into doing anything you don't feel comfortable with.

8. Take time to evaluate things. Even if things go really well on the first date, try to keep your feelings under control. Give yourself time to digest everything before you make plans for the next date. This is an excellent time to talk with a friend who went along on the first date (if you were able to arrange a double date or a small-group activity).

Assessing Your First Date

When you get home from your first date, it's likely you'll experience one of three feelings: (1) a post-date high, (2) post-date depression, or (3) indifference. Here's what each feeling might signal about your relationship:

A post-date high. Nothing will be more exciting than for a first date to confirm all of your best hopes. People become electrified when they discover that their date truly is charming and funny and attractive and articulate. Who wouldn't be high after having coffee with such a person? But while you're floating on clouds during dessert, pinching yourself because your online date is even more impressive in person, resist having a conversation about long-term commitments. Just end the date on a positive note and go home. Give yourself time to process what happened, what was said, how you felt, and where God is leading from here. If you can, bring a friend into this private evaluation session. We all need a good sounding board.

Post-date depression. A post-date letdown is not uncommon, and it doesn't always mean that the first date was a bust. Instead, it may be that your expectations were unrealistic. If your date scored eight on a scale of one to ten, but you were expecting eleven out of ten, then stop and re-think your expectations. Whatever the reason was for your disappointment, analyze what happened. Don't let your unrealistic expectations make a pretty decent date seem like a train wreck. You might realize later that you shut the door on a perfectly acceptable person.

But maybe you found out that the person has been less than forth-right in e-mails and phone conversations. He suddenly pulls out pictures of his three kids (he has kids?!), or she sneezes and her false teeth pop out. If your match failed to mention such details earlier, what other details might he or she have "forgotten" to mention?

Or maybe it wasn't a matter of dishonesty, but just a matter of meeting and observing the person for the first time. Maybe the guy can't stop picking his nails, or the woman keeps tossing her hair and checking her lipstick, and you just want to scream. Maybe the guy whips out his cell phone to call his mother, or the woman reveals that she voted for a pres-idential candidate you can't stand.

If you're feeling low, for whatever reason, give yourself time to analyze your feelings and understand what that means for your relationship. You can correct your own unrealistic expectations if that's the basic problem. Annoying habits and quirks are another matter. You have to decide how much they really bother you. And finding out details that should have been disclosed prior to your first face-to-face meeting is another thing entirely.

Indifference. This is the reaction that falls between the exhilaration of a great date and the disappointment of a bust. Many times competing emotions will leave you confused. You may be extremely attracted to the person online and can't figure out why you are so much less enthusiastic about him or her in person. There may be no fatal flaw, just nothing that quickens your pulse. He or she may be a great match—but for someone else.

Give serious thought to the reasons for your indifference. Maybe you just need to spend more time together so you can make a better decision.

Freda, an office manager from Detroit, almost blew it when she felt indifferent after her first in-person date with Scott.

"It was obvious that he was really attracted to me," she says, "and I couldn't put my finger on why I was less than thrilled. He wasn't quite the same as he was online, and when we met I felt like I might be settling too soon. I got home and started praying about my feelings because Scott really was a nice, strong Christian man, and I didn't want to hurt him.

"I gave it another chance, and on our second date we had a much better time. I began to see more of what attracted me to him initially. Almost a year later, we married. I'm glad I didn't dump him just because I didn't get blown away by our first date."

DECIDING FOR OR AGAINST A SECOND DATE

After the first date, you have to decide whether to continue the relationship. If you're having serious doubts and it's clear that the other person was less than thrilled about the date, you might want to have the conversation right away. If a breakup is imminent, there's no reason to put it off.

If, however, you're feeling indifferent, you need time to think. But don't take too long to make a decision. The other person is waiting to hear how you're feeling. Show him or her some consideration, and don't wait more than a day or two before you call.

If you have to break up with someone, then make it known in real time—either in person or by telephone if you live a great distance apart. Show respect for the other person and give the relationship proper closure.

But you may not need that advice at all. If both of you were blown away by your first date and can't wait to spend more time together, congratulations! Now that you're an offline couple, you can move ahead in confirming that this is the person God wants you to marry. Try to spend time with each other in a wide variety of activities, including some ministry involvement, so you can see how the other person handles different situations.

There is no need to rush. You have come a long way in your relationship, and shared experiences over time should only make your relationship stronger—and let you know beyond a doubt whether this person truly is "the one" for you.

Navigating Your World Wide Search

God, Prayer, Wisdom—Don't Log On Without Them

Don't pay attention to the skeptics. It is possible to find the love of your life online.

Those who are savvy enough to understand the limitations and possibilities, the pitfalls and the blessings of this approach begin the process with practiced skills and a clear plan. They keep their expectations realistic and stay plugged in to their offline support network.

As you date online, stay in tune with the prompting of the Holy Spirit. Seek God's guidance as you make decisions about moving the relationship to the next stage or bailing out.

If you marry someone you met online, don't listen to those who treat your marriage like it's somehow substandard just because you met each other on the Internet. Seek support instead from those who understand you and your relationship. You know that the online dating process is nothing like a virtual singles bar or a matchmaking meat market. So talk to others about your positive experiences. Other singles who seek relationships online will benefit from the lessons you have learned.

If you try online dating and discover that the process just doesn't work for you, remember that God is still in control of your search for a spouse. Online dating is just one tool available to you. Continue to live your life in joyful service to the Lord, and continue to meet people in your existing social networks.

Your life is in God's hands. Conduct your search for a spouse both offline and in cyberspace as if you really believe it. Your choices will be blessed as a result.

Notes

Prologue

1. Amy Harmon, "Online Dating Sheds Its Stigma as Losers.com," *New York Times* (29 June 2003).
2. Amber L. Anderson, "Surf Here Often?" *Christianity Today* (11 June 2001). Found at www.christianitytoday.com/ct/2001/008/3.38.html.
3. *El Paso Times,* "Clicking for Love: Online Connection Ends in Marriage" (11 January 2003): 3.
4. N. R. Kleinfield, "An Officer and a Gentleman? 50 Women Would Disagree," *New York Times* (11 June 2003).
5. Michael Rogers, "The Secrets of Online Romance," *Newsweek Online* (1 October 2002). Article ID: 100102_rogers_romance.
6. Tom Geoghegan, "We Found Love Online," *BBC News Online* (25 November 2002). Found at http://news.bbc.co.uk/1/hi/uk/2508793.stm.
7. Geoghegan, "We Found Love Online."

Chapter 2

1. Mark Wolf, "Eharmony Lets Lovelorn Click on Reality," *Rocky Mountain News* (22 June 2002).

Chapter 3

1. Joyce Cohen, "On the Net, Love Really Is Blind," *New York Times* (18 January 2001).

Chapter 6

1. Adapted, paraphrased, and abridged from a Seattle posting. But it could have been just about anyone on a dating Web site.

Chapter 7

1. I found out that Benny is from Kenya. Asking a question like this might be acceptable in his country, but in the United States, this question is offensive and guarantees that the person asking the question will receive no response.

Chapter 9

1. This does not necessarily mean that a person meets the clinical definition of having a certain psychological disorder.